About this Learning Guide

Shmoop Will Make You a Better Lover*
*of Literature, History, Poetry, Life...

Our lively learning guides are written by experts and educators who want to show your brain a good time. Shmoop writers come primarily from Ph.D. programs at top universities, including Stanford, Harvard, and UC Berkeley.

Want more Shmoop? We cover literature, poetry, bestsellers, music, US history, civics, biographies (and the list keeps growing). Drop by our website to see the latest.

www.shmoop.com

Table of Contents

Introduction

In a Nutshell

A Clockwork Orange was published in 1962 by Anthony Burgess. Interestingly, the book contained twenty-one chapters in its British debut, but only twenty chapters in its American release. Burgess was miffed about the decision by his New York publisher to "abridge" the book for its American audience, but he couldn't very well object at the time, as he was a starving writer. In any case, he got even eventually, when the book was re-released in 1986 in all of its twenty-one-chapter glory.

Unfortunately, Stanley Kubrick's movie bearing the same name was modeled after the slimmer American book release -- that is, the one without the final chapter. To Burgess's dismay, Kubrick's movie memorialized an incomplete version of his work. In any case, it turns out that Burgess actually didn't like his novel *A Clockwork Orange*, anyway. (Burgess liked it as much as Beethoven liked his Minuet in G, or Rachmaninoff his Prelude in C Sharp Minor, written when Rachmaninoff was a mere boy.)

Why Should I Care?

Come on, admit it. You're probably here because of the Stanley Kubrick movie, which, by the way, was adapted from this book and not vice versa. The hype is well-deserved, though, despite what Anthony Burgess himself had to say about it (in fact, he strongly disliked *A Clockwork Orange*, his book). There is a reason this book is still around after 40+ years. It is shocking. It is thrilling. It is innovative, and fashionable (in fact, the "heighth of fashion" described in the book can make New York Fashion Week look weak). What's more, this book addresses subculture, rebellion, music, teenage gangs, violence, rape, and slang – topics all still very relevant today, on the streets and in high schools alike. It really is the grand-daddy of edgy, and if you won't take our word for it, ask Stanley Kubrick.

Summary

Book Summary

A Clockwork Orange unfolds in the dark and chilly streets of a futuristic city. Alex, the 15-year-old leader of a violent teenage gang, narrates to us in an odd slang (nadsat, it is called) which takes some learning in the beginning.Alex introduces his entourage of criminals – Peter, Georgie, and Dim – and proceeds to take us on an eye-opening journey of ultra-violent crimes inflicted upon helpless innocent people. After boozing up at two local bars, the intoxicated Alex and Co. go on a rampage involving: mugging an old professor, a convenience store robbery, a rival gang fight, grand theft auto, a gang rape, vandalism, and arson. Back at the bar, Alex then gets into a fist fight with Dim and Georgie, who are unhappy with his arrogance. Tired, however, the gang retires for the night, leaving in their wake several hospitalizations, a wrecked car, a

good amount of road kill (thanks to their reckless driving), wrecked houses, emotional trauma, and a death.

The next day, Alex plays hooky, gets drunk, and rapes two 10-year-olds to the bombastic music of Beethoven's Symphony No. 9 . At night, he meets up with his friends and proceeds to break into an old woman's mansion to loot it. The police arrive in the nick of time and arrest Alex – just after Dim temporarily blinds Alex in the eye with his chain for payback. Sentenced to 14 years in jail, Alex initially has a hard time adjusting to the climate. Things get easier after two years, though, as he befriends the prison chaplain, takes an interest in the Bible, and is allowed to listen to classical music while doing Bible study.

A new cellmate, a filthy pervert, complicates things. When Alex and the other five cellmates beat their new colleague to death, Alex takes the fall for the murder. Consequently, Alex is chosen by the newly appointed Minister of the Interior to participate in a "reform" treatment called Ludovico's Technique, currently being tested. A behavioral-brainwashing procedure involving elements of associative learning, the treatment program lasts two weeks, after which the criminal is supposedly rendered completely unable to even think of committing crime. Alex is injected with a substance that makes him sick while being forced to watch violent films accompanied by classical music. As he comes to associate bodily sickness with violence, the mere thought of violence becomes so overwhelming to him that he'd rather suffer pain himself than have to think about inflicting pain upon others.

Released back into society as an innocuous person incapable of brutality, Alex returns home to his parents, only to be shooed out. He finds himself contemplating suicide at the public library, but victims of his criminal past find him and beat him up. When the police arrive to break up the fight, they turn out to be his old friends-turned-enemies, Dim and Billyboy, who also take him out to the countryside to get even. Left to die out in the snow, Alex wanders into a cottage; the good-hearted F. Alexander takes him in, bathes him, and feeds him.

F. Alexander turns out to be a political dissident hell-bent on overthrowing the current regime, having lost his wife to the ineffective Government two years ago. As he hears stories about the State's mistreatment of Alex, F. Alexander plans to use Alex as a weapon against the Government. Alex recognizes F. Alexander as the writer-husband of the woman he gang-raped two years ago. It takes a while for F. Alexander to recognize Alex, but he eventually does, by the strange way Alex speaks (his use of the slang language, nadsat).

Alex is locked away by F. Alexander's associates in an apartment. The men blast classical music through the wall, seeking to drive Alex to suicide so as to better indict the Government. Alex, driven mad by the sad side-effect of Ludovico's Technique, jumps from the window of the apartment, but he doesn't die. When he comes to in a few weeks time, the State has undone Alex's Reclamation Treatment, F. Alexander has been locked away, a great job has been lined up for Alex, and the Minister of the Interior makes peace with him by presenting him with a new stereo.

Back to his old self, Alex hangs out with a new gang – Len, Rick, and Bully – that engages in some of the same violent behavior as his old group. Somehow, though, Alex is discontent with his lifestyle. A chance encounter with his old friend, Pete, and Pete's new wife, Georgina, at a

local coffeehouse arouses a renewed interest in Alex for a "normal" life. Alex resolves that he wants a wife and son for himself, too, and decides that he'll take steps toward attaining that dream.

Part One, Chapter One

- "What's it going to be then, eh?" That's how the book opens, and you'll find this question dispersed throughout; it will even close with it, coming full circle. The significance, you ask? Well, we like to think of it as a "marker" of some significance. See if you can figure it out before we tell you.
- Our narrator and protagonist, Alex, along with his "droogs" (that would be "friends"), Pete, Georgie, and Dim, are sitting in the Korova Milkbar contemplating what trouble to get into on this particularly dark and chilly winter evening.
- Alex and his entourage are drinking "milk-plus," which means milk laced with some type of hallucinogen or other drug. Alex describes the milk-plus experience as one that either gives you a nice fireworks-in-the-sky kind of buzz, or a lot of courage and strength.
- The entourage has a lot of "deng," or money, so there's no real need to get "ultra-violent" with an old guy or gal in the alley for the dough. After all, as they say, money isn't everything.
- Alex describes his entourage as dressed in the "heighth of fashion," which, at the time, means a pair of black tights, a big belt, a cropped jacket without lapels but with big, built-up shoulders, a hat, and great boots for kicking.
- Alex observes three girls at the bar also dressed in the "heighth of fashion," what with expensive colorful wigs on, makeup to match, and long black dresses with badges displaying the names of men they've had sex with before they turned fourteen attached. That's right, you heard him, age fourteen.
- The man sitting next to Alex is quite drunk and talking gibberish about Aristotle. Not amused at all, Alex finds it rather cowardly that this grown dude next to him could get so wasted.
- The milk-plus starts to kick in for our boys. How do we know? Well, when you start to hear voices moving from one part of the bar to another, "flying up to the ceiling and then swooping down again and whizzing from wall to wall," and when you "feel the knives in the old moloko starting to prick," you just know.
- "Out out out out!" Alex shouts, and the entourage leaves the bar for Marghanita Boulevard.
- They turn down Boothby Avenue, looking for trouble.
- AHA! The first victim of the night has been identified as an old, bespectacled, schoolmaster type guy who is hurrying down the street from the public library, with books tucked under one arm and a crappy umbrella hanging on the other.
- Alex approaches him, calling him "brother," but otherwise speaking in proper English instead of the nadsat we've been exposed to since the second line of the book.
- Pete confiscates the old man's books and passes them around: Elementary Crystallography, The Miracle of the Snowflake, and The Rhombohedral System. Flipping through one of them, Alex insinuates that it's a book of pornography, and teases the man about it.
- The man tries to grab his books back with futility.
- Alex decides that the gesture warrants teaching him a little lesson.

- The boys hold the man back, and each takes a turn beating him about the head. They then rip off his glasses, tear out his false teeth, and kick him about until "out comes the blood… real beautiful." They strip him of his clothes. A final kick in the stomach, and they let the man stagger off.
- The boys now go through his trousers for money, also finding a few old handwritten letters.
- The boys are off to the Duke of New York bar on Amis Avenue to spend what money they have robbed the from the old teacher.
- They come upon three or four old ladies at the bar – really drunk – and buy them drinks and snacks in exchange for an alibi. The "baboochkas" seem very happy about the exchange.
- The boys leave the bar for this cigs and sweets shop on the corner of Attlee Avenue. Apparently, this shop was a regular "job" for these boys, and the fact that it's been left alone for three months now means that some money is due.
- The boys put on their high-quality, life-like masks, each one the face of a historical personality: Alex has Disraeli, Pete has Elvis Presley, Georgie has Henry VIII, and Dim wears P. B. Shelley, the poet.
- Barging inside the store, the boys go for Slouse, the shopkeeper, before he has time to ring the police or grab his gun. Alex beats up Mother Slouse, the wife of the shopkeeper, kicking her, ripping her clothes, staring at her naked breasts, even contemplating sex until resolving that this is for later on in the evening.
- The boys clean the register, grab a few packs of the very best cigarettes (they call them "cancers"), and jet back to the Duke of New York in less than ten minutes altogether.
- The boys buy the alibi ladies more drinks.
- Half an hour passes before the police come to question the patrons of the bar for potential information. Apparently, the Slouses have needed hospitalization.
- The boys sneer at the police, all the while the ladies provide them with their purchased alibi.

Part One, Chapter Two

- Outside of the Duke of New York, the boys encounter a singing drunk. Even after a few tastes of the fist, the drunk continues to sing about the "stinking world" he lives in, lamenting how violent youths like Alex and posse rule, with no deference to law and order.
- The drunk guy burps.
- And of course, he gets a bloody beating from Alex and co.
- Alex's posse moves on and comes upon Billyboy and his five droogs right around the Municipal Power Plant. Billyboy and his entourage are getting ready to rape a weepy young girl, probably not more than ten years of age.
- Alex notes that "teaming up" these days is like forming an "auto-team," with four being a comfortable number for an auto, and six being on the "outside limit for gang-size." Anyway, it is Alex4 against Billyboy6.
- Alex hates how Billyboy always smells like stale oil, and challenges him and his entourage to a fight.
- Dim has a great chain he's using on these opponents, while George and Pete both wield

sharp knives. Alex also puts his cut-throat knife to use, slitting open the front of one of his opponent's jackets and leaving him bare bellied…

- The fight grows bloody in the dark, with Dim coming out the worst in looks, his body all bloodied. Billyboy doesn't look so hot either, particularly after Alex cuts both sides of his cheeks until two curtains of blood pour out at the same time.
- Like Dim, Billyboy doesn't feel a thing. Because they're big, dim, and tough like that.
- Anyhow, of course Alex and Co. are coming out on top in the fight…until they hear sirens.
- No doubt the little ten-year-old has tattled.
- All the boys scatter. Alex and friends run to a dark alley to catch their breath. They look up at the stars, the moon, and the blue light emitted by hundreds of television sets in the apartments above. All these light-emitting things fascinate Dim, but Alex just gets annoyed.
- With the sirens gone, Alex leads his friends to Priestley Place, then to the Filmdrome (theatre) parking lot to look for a getaway car.
- They steal a new-ish Durango 95 easily, thanks to Georgie's little tool that he keeps on his keychain.
- The boys drive recklessly, puffing on the cancers left in the backseat, ramming into couples trying to get it on in their cars, running over animals large and small, and just generally terrorizing the townspeople.
- The moon shines brightly as Alex decides that it's time for the "old surprise visit." Driving into the countryside, he stops the car just before entering "a sort of a village," in front of a small cottage that has "HOME" on a plate hanging on the gate.
- Alex knocks on the door of the cottage; a woman answers.
- Speaking like a gentleman, Alex asks to use the phone to call an ambulance for his friend, who supposedly has fallen ill just outside the cottage.
- The woman says that she doesn't own a telephone.
- Alex asks for a glass of water to soothe his friend.
- The woman, fooled by Alex's gentlemanly speech, goes off to fetch it without locking the door.
- Alex and co. put on their masks and barge in.
- They observe that the woman has great boobs and her husband is a young writer, wearing horn-rimmed glasses.
- The writer protests.
- Alex, picking up a pile of typewriter paper, starts to mock the writer. "A CLOCKWORK ORANGE" is the title of the manuscript… Alex continues to read on, until Dim starts to get bored, at which point Alex tears up the manuscript.
- The writer lashes out at Alex. Dim starts to beat up the writer.
- Georgie and Pete return to the living room, stuffing their faces with food they've hoarded in the kitchen.
- Alex orders Georgie and Pete to drop the food and grab the writer so he can watch what's about to be done.
- Dim holds the writer's wife down, while Alex begins to rip off her clothes.
- Her boobs are real nice with their pink nipples.
- Excited, Alex gets undressed and starts to "plunge." Cries of agony and pain are heard and the writer howls the dirtiest of words at him.
- Alex finishes, and Dim takes his turn with the woman while Alex holds her down.
- Then Pete and Georgie have their turns with her.
- After the gang rape, the boys get really crazy, smashing up everything in the cottage,

burning and pissing on things. Just as Dim prepares to take a dump on the carpet, Alex howls, "Out out out out!"

- The tired Alex lets Georgie take the wheel of the waiting car. The gang heads back to town, running over odd animals here and there.

Part One, Chapter Three

- Running out of fuel, the boys abandon the Durango, pushing it into the wasteland waters. They catch the train. It's interesting to note that there are slot machines on board. Despite paying the fare nice and polite and like perfect gentlemen, irony abounds when the boys start tearing up the curtains and the upholstery of the seats on the train. They do a lot of damage on their three-minute ride.
- The boys get off at Center station and walk back to Korova Milkbar.
- Tired, they realize they should get home soon, since they're still growing boys with school the next day. Did you catch that? These boys are really boys!
- The Korova seems different from the way they left it earlier in the evening.
- For one, except for the drunkard who's still there, there are now many more "nadsats" (or teens) at the bar.
- Opera music is playing, and one of the women in her late thirties sings along. Alex, being very sensitive to classical music, shivers upon hearing it.
- Dim interrupts Alex's moment with a bit of vulgarity, causing Alex to cuss him out.
- Not enough, apparently, Alex leans over Georgie to punch Dim in the mouth.
- Dim, hurt, confronts Alex.
- Alex chastises him for being a "bastard with no manners."
- Dim says he doesn't want to be Alex's brother and friend anymore.
- Asserting his authority, Alex challenges Dim to a fight outside.
- Dim gets a bit riled up.
- Pete tries to break up the fight about to ensue between these friends.
- Alex retorts that Dim has to learn his place, since Alex is the leader.
- Unconvinced, Georgie steps in and tries to appease Alex.
- Pete says to Alex that his punching Dim was uncalled for.
- An impassioned Alex re-asserts his leadership and authority, stating that even among friends, somebody has to be in charge. Alex explains his intolerance for any interference with operatic singing that he so enjoys.
- Surprisingly, Dim seems to suddenly click, and suggests that everyone drop the argument and just go home.
- Same time and place tomorrow night? Yes.
- Alone now, Alex walks back to his parents' flat at 18A, Municipal Flatblock, between Kingsley Avenue and Wilsonsway. Along the way, he passes by one teenage boy, all beat up and bloody, and two young girls, who've just been raped, no doubt.
- The elevator is broken again, and freshly so, it appears.
- Alex takes the stairs, finally arriving on the 18th floor to a dark and quiet apartment.
- Alex gulps up the milk and dinner that have been laid out for him.
- After brushing his teeth, he enters his bedroom to sleep.

- He looks proudly at the flags and manners on the walls, his many music discs and stereo... He puts on some classical music, and finds instantaneous bliss. He finally drifts off to dreamland to some J.S. Bach, with thoughts about a clockwork orange.
- From the beautiful descriptions of the colors and sounds Alex sees and experiences, we wouldn't be surprised if Burgess has intended a synesthetic experience for our character. (Synesthesia is seeing certain colors when hearing specific sounds.)

Part One, Chapter Four

- Alex comes to at 8am and feels pretty bad physically.
- His mother enters the room, urging him to go to school.
- Alex responds that he has a headache and wants to sleep it off instead. Umm, can you say, hooky?
- Mom puts his breakfast in the oven and hurries off to her job as a stocker of shelves at a supermarket.
- Alex drifts back to dreamland, and has a nightmare in which Georgie is a powerful commander general indicting him for one crime or another. Then Dim runs after Alex and beats him up.
- Alex wakes up with his heart palpitating fast. The doorbell goes off.
- At the door is P. R. Deltoid, Alex's Post-Corrective Adviser, stopping by to check up on him.
- Alex explains that he has ditched school because of a rather intolerable pain in the head, and offers P. R. Deltoid some tea.
- P. R. Deltoid declines the tea, stating that there's no time for it, and proceeds to play some word/mind-game with Alex. He warns Alex that he had better stay out of trouble, or he's going to go to jail if he gets caught.
- Alex denies that he's done anything worthy of worry. Yeah, right.
- P. R. Deltoid responds that he's privy to a fair amount of nastiness that occurred last night, and that Alex's name had been mentioned. So, even if the police can't prove anything about anybody, Alex has been forewarned.
- P. R. Deltoid muses out loud that Alex has a loving home, a great set of parents, and isn't dumb, but why oh why has he turned out this way?
- Alex continues with the "I don't know what you're talking about" approach.
- After P. R. Deltoid leaves, Alex dismisses his warnings as silly. He now muses over the concepts of goodness and badness, and wonders out loud that modern youths like himself commit crimes for the sheer enjoyment of it. Alex then waxes philosophical, concluding that if his government does not allow bad behavior, then it denies its constituents a life to live and, by definition, ceases to be a government at all.
- Alex has his breakfast and reads the paper. The usual ultra-violence, bank robberies, and strikes litter the news. A certain article on modern youth amuses him, but he dismisses most of its analyses as stupid and without insight.
- Alex recalls reading and liking one article by a certain clergyman who claims the devil is responsible for the ultra-violent modern youth. Finding that this theory conveniently absolves him of any moral responsibility, Alex approves.

- Alex gets dressed with the radio playing. A familiar string quartet plays and Alex is overjoyed. He thinks about another article he once read, about how appreciation for the arts and music could make modern youth more civilized. Alex totally agrees.
- On his way out to the record store to pick up a copy of Beethoven's Symphony No. 9, Alex notes that the day differs greatly from the night. The night belongs to young folks like him, the day to old fogies and the policemen that protect them.
- Alex gets to Melodia, the record store, at Taylor Place and eyes the two ten-year-old girls in there, who are also playing hooky.
- He asks the storekeeper, old Andy, for Beethoven's Ninth.
- While paying for his new record, one of the pop music girls flirts with Alex. Alex gets an idea in his head, and promptly flirts back, promising food and music if they'll leave with him.
- Alex buys the girls, named Marty and Sonietta, spaghetti, sausages, cream-puffs, banana-splits, and hot chocolate. Then he orders a taxi to bring them back to Municipal Flatblock 18A.
- At his parents' flat, Alex gives the girls a lot of Scotch and plays for them the pop music they brought. He encourages them to drink more, and quickly.
- By the time their discs have been spun two times, the girls are thoroughly drunk, hyped up, and jumping on Alex's beds.
- Alex puts on Beethoven's Ninth and leaps on the girls, raping them to the joyous tunes of "Ode to Joy."
- The Ninth goes on repeat, too, and by the time Alex is finished with the girls, they are no longer so happy and hyped up, but rather bruised and pouty. (Wow, those ten-year-olds sure handled it well.)
- Alex lets them gather their things and kicks them out of the flat. He promptly dozes off to more "Ode to Joy."

Part One, Chapter Five

- It is almost 7:30 p.m. when Alex awakes. His stereo has stopped, which meant that his parents probably turned it off when they got home.
- Putting on his coat, he peers out, bidding his parents hello as the loving only-son to them.
- Alex takes a shower, and joins his parents at the dinner table.
- His father asks about his night job.
- Alex responds that it's just odd things, here and there. He also makes the point that he never asks for spending money.
- Appeased, his father talks about a nightmare he had about Alex, beaten and lying in the street.
- Alex assures him that he's not up to no good. He reaches in his pockets and puts some money on the table, offering it to his parents to buy some Scotch at a bar.
- The parents accept Alex's nice gesture, but decline to go out since the streets are too dangerous because of the modern youth.
- By the time Alex gets to the bottom of the stairs of Municipal Flatblock, his droogs are already waiting…yes, dressed in the heighth of fashion.

- The entourage lets Alex know that it got worried when he was late.
- Alex recounts his day: headache, then the visit from P. R. Deltoid, conveniently leaving out the girls.
- Georgie gets sarcastic with Alex, or so Alex charges.
- Alex goes on a rant about leadership and sarcasm, and insults Dim meanwhile.
- Georgie defends Dim, asking Alex not to pick on him again, staying that there is a "new way" to which the posse has agreed.
- Alex gets flippant. New way? No way.
- Pete chimes in and says that the posse wants things to be more democratic. Instead of Alex making the calls all the time, they ought to be able to voice and do what they want to do.
- Georgie announces that he has a "mansize" plan for tonight.
- Seeing that he is outnumbered, Alex smiles and plays along, asking Georgie about his plan.
- Georgie says that the gang should sharpen up with some spiked milk first, and starts to lead the way to the Korova.
- Alex hears Beethoven's Violin Concerto on the radio of a passing car, and he feels a violent surge in his veins. He draws his knife on Georgie.
- Georgie draws his knife, and the two have at it until Alex cuts Georgie's hand.
- Now Dim uncoils his chain and lunges at Alex. Alex gets hit on the back, but manages to get back up and slash Dim's left wrist. Blood gushes out like a fountain.
- Alex challenges a worried Pete. Pete is afraid that Dim's going to bleed to death.
- The emerging leader, Alex, now binds Dim's wrist with some cloth in his pocket. Declaring himself master and leader again, Alex gets his friends to the Duke of New York for a calm time.
- They see the alibi ladies, who are ultra-friendly with them.
- Alex confirms with Georgie that all is forgotten.
- Georgie suggests that his "mansize" plan for the night is to rob the Mansion (or the Manse), where a very old woman lives with her cats and valuables.
- Alex agrees that it's a great idea.
- Alex promises the alibi girls more drinks when they get back in ten minutes.
- Giving us a bit of foreshadowing, Alex says he "led [his] three droogs out to [his] doom."

Part One, Chapter Six

- Going east from the Duke of New York, one would first come upon the business district, then the library, then an apartment complex named Victoria Flatblock, and, finally, Oldtown, where the houses are quite ancient.
- The Manse is the site for the night's job. It's a big place, with multiple stories, barred windows, and even globe lights guarding the front door.
- Judging from the milk saucers around the property, everyone in town knows this place to be a sanctuary for cats. In fact, if you were to stay long enough, you would see them jumping around in the house. You could also see the old woman talking to the cats in her mansion.

- The boys plan how to obtain access. They will try the old plan of the fainted friend to get in the door and wreak havoc.
- Alex, anxious to prove himself as a worthwhile leader, runs with the plan.
- Instead of being another easy victim, the woman threatens to shoot if they don't leave.
- Alex pleads that she help his ill-fallen friend.
- The woman threatens to unleash her cats on him.
- Alex pretends to retreat, all the while narrating how the woman's suspicions are well founded since the streets are a dangerous place.
- In the dark, the gang reconvenes. Alex, still anxious to show them who's who, suggests that he stand on Dim's shoulders to open a window for all.
- The plan works! Alex cracks the glass and hops into a room full of beds, cupboards, boxes, and books.
- Once inside, Alex decides that he'll do the job (which includes robbing, raping, and possibly killing) alone to impress his droogs...so they could really learn all about leadership when he opens the front door bearing all the valuables.
- Eyeing the stairs going down to the hall, Alex waltzes down there and startles the cat-lady.
- The place is full of cats, and the air filled with floating fur. (Umm, Cruella, is that you?)
- Cat-woman raises her walking-stick at Alex. Alex gets distracted by a stone bust of Beethoven.
- Not seeing the milk saucers on the floor, he trips.
- WHACK! Cat-lady cracks his head with her stick.
- Alex grabs her stick and pulls her down on the floor, still holding onto the table-cloth.
- The cats jump everywhere. Alex steps on the tail of one and it bites and claws his leg.
- More struggling ensues on the floor as Alex tries to get up. The cat-lady summons her cats to attack Alex. Tripping on another milk saucer, Alex is down, being scratched by the cats and whacked on the head by their owner's walking stick.
- Fed up, Alex takes a silver statue and bashes the cat-lady across the head with it. She shuts up immediately.
- Police sirens sound in the distance. Alex runs for the front door.
- He is met with Dim and Dim's chain.
- Dim whips Alex in the head with his chain, blinding him momentarily, and then runs off.
- Alex stumbles in the hallway, groping at things blindly, until the policemen come upon him.
- The policemen know his name, and taunt him violently.
- Alex realizes that Dim and co. have sold him out.
- Alex yells at the police that his friends – his former brothers – forced him to do this. He then realizes that tattling on them will do no good, since they've probably already escaped to safety at the Duke of New York and are getting chummy with the alibi ladies.
- Wedged in between two policemen, Alex is taken away in the squad car, still kind of blind from Dim's chain and seeing the city go by as a blur.
- An ambulance goes the other way, and one of the policemen informs us that it is for the cat-lady.
- Alex insists that his friends put him up to the test with this last job.
- The policemen, knowing full well the exploits of the famous Alex, assure him that he's got the whole evening to tell the story of how his friends led him astray.

Part One, Chapter Seven

- Alex is dragged into a brightly lit office with whitewashed walls. It smells like vomit and piss and bleach. Sounds of agony from other prisoners penetrate the walls. Alex finds himself among four policemen, all of them sipping strong tea.
- Alex demands a lawyer, but gets laughed at and punched instead.
- Alex almost throws up, but holds it back.
- Alex retaliates with a kick and punch.
- After that, though, the four policemen gang up on him and beat him until he cries out apologies.
- P. R. Deltoid comes to visit, unamused.
- He looks at Alex as if he were a thing and no longer a boy.
- Alex tries to explain that he was duly influenced by his no-good friends.
- Coldly, P. R. Deltoid promises to appear in court tomorrow.
- The other policemen urge P. R. Deltoid to give Alex a bash in the chops, but instead he pulls his face close to Alex's and spits full in Alex's face. He then wipes his wet lips with the back of his hand. Alex thanks P. R. Deltoid, who leaves promptly.
- The police now push Alex to make a statement, to be turned into a signed confession. So, Alex gushes about the ultra-violence and the rape for pages on end, making sure to include his so-called friends.
- Alex is then kicked, punched, and bullied off to a holding cell with ten or twelve other criminals, most of them drunk. Two of these criminals are "queer" and immediately try to molest him. Alex manages to fight them off with the help of a cop.
- Exhausted, Alex drifts off thinking about Beethoven's Ninth.
- A cop comes to wake Alex up from the other end of the holding cell. Reluctantly, Alex goes to him.
- But before the cop opens his mouth, Alex guesses it: the cat-lady has died in the hospital; apparently, Alex cracked her a bit too hard.
- Alex thinks about all the cats, now orphaned, having no mistress who will feed them.
- Alex realizes that he has committed murder, and reveals that he has done so at the ripe old age of fifteen.

Part Two, Chapter One

- What's it going to be then, eh?
- Alex narrates from cell number 84F in Staja (that's short for State Jail), two years after his sentencing.
- After a lot of "slander" and testimony by P.R. Deltoid and the cops, Alex is apparently sentenced to fourteen years; his mother howled.
- Now dressed in the "heighth" of prison fashion – that would be a jumpsuit in a filthy "poop-color" – known only by the prisoner number "6655321" that adorns it, Alex no longer feels like himself. (Wait, is that Burgess being cliché?)
- Alex reflects upon the two hard years in the human zoo. On a daily basis, he has dealt with wardens that kick and beat him, perverts who wish to rape him, all the while toiling away in

the factory making matchboxes and doing exercises in the courtyard. Sometimes, he has to suffer through guest speeches on beetles or the Milky Way for "education" purposes, but during these speeches, he keeps himself entertained thinking about happier, ultraviolent days.

- One day, Alex is informed that his friend Georgie died while involved in some ultraviolence with Dim and Pete. Alex is glad that fate made sure that traitorous Georgie did not live a happy or long life.
- More time passes, and Alex adjusts to prison life. He has a new job playing the stereo for the prison chaplain during Sunday worship. He likes his new job because it involves music. (Wow, we would have never seen that coming.)
- One day during Sunday worship, some dude in the back lets out a burp and is quickly kicked, beaten, and dragged out of the church.
- The chaplain goes on without a glitch.
- Alex reveals that the chaplain likes him because of his interest in the Bible. Alex especially delights in all the sex and violence he gets to read about in the Old Testament. The icing on the cake is that the chaplain lets him listen to holy music by Bach and Handel while he reads pages upon pages of ultraviolence! What a deal.
- Alex is not so partial to the New Testament because it gets all preachy on him. Of course, the one part of the NT he does enjoy is the part where he imagines himself whipping and nailing Jesus to the cross. Yikes.
- Alex is good at his new job, always ready with the record or the disc on queue, no matter what commotion ensues in the main worship room.
- One Sunday after the service, the prison chaplain speaks with Alex about the various goings-on in the prison. Apparently, the prison chaplain is looking for a huge promotion, and in order to get a good recommendation from the Governor, he occasionally provides the Governor with underground information about the prisoners – underground information that he gets from Alex the Snitch, though Alex mostly just makes it up.
- This time, Alex tells the prison chaplain that some consignment of cocaine has arrived and is going to be distributed to the various prisoners. Of course, this is false, but hey, who cares about the truth if the recipients prefer the lie?
- Alex takes the chance to ask the chaplain if he appreciates his help. The chaplain answers in the affirmative.
- Now is the time. Alex asks about a certain new "treatment" that allows one to get out of prison in no time at all, while ensuring he stay out of prison as well.
- Ludovico's Technique, answers the chaplain thoughtfully, hesitantly cautioning Alex that the program is in its infancy.
- Alex answers that it must be starting to see some use, because he sees the new white buildings they've been building adjacent to the Staja.
- The chaplain answers that it has not been put to use yet, and that there are grave doubts about whether any technique can really reform a man and make him good.
- The chat ends abruptly when the chaplain orders Alex to Bible study.
- Alex goes back to his cell after lunch to find that he has a new cellmate. The cell was built for only three prisoners, but now has seven of them crammed in, sweaty and tight.

Part Two, Chapter Two

- Alex muses that his new cellmate marked the beginning of his getting out of jail.
- This new guy's a bit of an arrogant shmuck, trying to make the argument that because he's youngest, Alex ought to sleep on the floor and give up his bed.
- Alex's other cellmates defend him.
- That night, Alex wakes up to find the new guy lying next to him in his bed, snoring and masturbating! Alex punches him as a part of a reflex.
- The other cellmates wake up and join in, beating up the perverted shmuck.
- The brawl causes the lights to be turned on, and the guards arrive to find the newest guy all bloody.
- Everyone points to Alex being the fire starter. Alex complains that he's not going to tolerate a horrible stinking perverted shmuck to molest him in his sleep.
- The guards make fun of him for being a princess and leave after turning the lights off.
- In the dark, the prisoners chat and decide that they'll teach the new cellmate a lesson.
- They throw fists and punches at him, and Alex ends it by kicking him in the head. Apparently, he drifts off into sleep.
- Alex goes to bed, dreaming about Beethoven and Handel until the prison buzzer wakes him up.
- The victim of last night's violence is lying on the floor, face down in a pool of blood.
- Alex touches his stiff body and pronounces him dead.
- The prisoners panic a bit, but decide that Alex is the main person responsible for his death.
- Alex retorts that everyone joined in on teaching the shmuck a lesson, so why should he take the fall?
- He is reminded of the time two years ago when his so-called droogs left him to the brutal cops. Is there no trust anywhere in the world?
- The dead body is soon carried off and the prison locked up until further notice by the Governor.
- At 11am, the Governor and the Chief and other important-looking officials come for Alex. They chat amongst themselves about whether the Government ought to move away from outmoded penological theories and embrace the new theory proposed from a "curative" view.
- Alex tries to butt in, but is shut down quickly.
- One of the official looking people turns to the Governor and suggests he take Alex to Brodsky, because Alex is young, bold, and vicious… and ought to be transformed out of recognition.
- To Alex, those words seem to offer the sweet taste of freedom.

Part Two, Chapter Three

- That evening, the guards drag Alex down to the Governor's office.
- The Governor informs him that the important man who graced his cell in the morning was the new Minister of the Interior, who apparently has odd ideas about the state reform system.

- The Governor tells Alex that he is to be "transformed" starting tomorrow by enrolling in a two-week program which will end in his release.
- Alex expresses his gratitude.
- The Governor tells him to save it, because the Reclamation Treatment is far from being a reward. (Is that foreshadowing?)
- Alex signs a waiver granting the State the power to "reclaim" him.
- The prison chaplain wants a word with Alex in his office.
- Drunk on Scotch and smoking a cancer, he waxes philosophical with Alex. Ethics, moral compulsion, desire to commit violence, free will, choice and many other topics come pouring out of his mouth. He questions the viability of a program which seeks to remove freedom of choice from a criminal. He wonders whether it is ungodly to become a person who would be deprived of the ability to make an ethical choice, because prayer would no longer be able to reach him.
- Their conversation ends when the chaplain breaks out in a hymn.
- The next morning, the guards bring Alex to the new white building adjacent to Staja, punching and kicking him all the way there.
- The building has a very hospital-like feel to it, and Alex is passed from one white coat to another until he comes to his white clean room, with curtains, a bedside lamp, and just one bed in it… all for Alex.
- Alex feels lucky.
- He changes out of his prison jumpsuit and receives a green set of pajamas, at the "heighth" of bed-wear fashion. Nice!
- Alex sips coffee, he is given magazines to browse.
- Dr. Branom, who is Dr. Brodsky's assistant, comes in to meet Alex and give him a brief examination.
- Alex asks what he'll be doing.
- Dr. Branom tells him that it's a simple treatment involving films.
- Films?
- Yes, special films. The first session commences this afternoon.
- Dr. Branom decides that Alex seems a bit under-nourished, probably due to prison food.
- He suggests that Alex expect a shot after every meal.
- A shot of vitamins?
- You know, something like that.
- Alex lies in bed daydreaming about freedom, getting out, and getting a new gang together.
- He has a meal of hot roast beef with mashed potatoes, and ice cream and tea for dessert. There's even a cigarette.
- This is the life, Alex thinks.
- Half an hour after his meal, a woman nurse with nice breasts comes in and gives him a shot in the arm.
- Some white coat now comes in with a wheelchair for Alex. Alex questions why it's necessary.
- He realizes soon after that he's feeling a bit weak, probably from the under-nourishment he suffered in prison. He is confident that the vitamins in the injection will put him on his A-game soon enough.

Part Two, Chapter Four

- Alex enters a mind-blowing room. A silver screen runs the length of one wall. Opposite that is a wall with square holes for projectors. Speakers are ubiquitous. Against another wall is a panel of meters. A dentist-looking chair with all sorts of wires poking out sits in the middle of the floor, facing the silver screen.
- Still feeling weak, Alex has to crawl from the wheelchair into the dentist's chair.
- Underneath the projection holes, he notices a panel of frosted glass with shadows of people moving behind it.
- A white coat straps his head, hands, and feet down; the personnel also attach clips to his forehead so that his eyelids are forced to remain open.
- Alex wonders out loud how "horrorshow" this film must be.
- Dr. Brodsky enters the room. Short, fat, bespectacled, flat-nosed, and with curly hair, he also has a suit that's absolutely the heighth of fashion.
- In a very breathy voice, Dr. Brodsky gives the go, after which the lights are turned off and everything else is switched on.
- The first film opens with an atmosphere of discord – no title, no credits, eerie music, a dark street…an old man walking down that street is attacked by two young guys dressed in the heighth of fashion. His screams and blood seem very realistic. Alex begins to feel ill in the stomach.
- He tries to forget about the nausea and focus on the second film. Six or seven malchicks (boys) are raping a young girl. Her screaming was so pathetic, and the tragic music playing adds to the "real" effect. Alex wonders about the kind of tricks used in making the movie seem so real; or are these actual snuff films?
- Alex feels pain all over his body, also wanting to throw up one minute and not the next. He begins to feel distress.
- Dr. Brodsky stands over the panel of switches gauging his reaction to be about 12.5 on the meter. He notes that this is promising for Alex.
- A third film is shown. This one has a face being held still and cut with a razor. Alex feels heavy sweat drip down his throbbing head and experiences a lot of pain in his stomach. The film goes on to show how a razor cuts out the man's eye and how pliers yank out all of his teeth. Alex reasons with himself that this film could not be real, but he still feels just as sick. At this point, Dr. Brodsky says "Excellent" three times, still monitoring the meters.
- A fourth film shows an old woman shopkeeper being robbed by a lot of modern youth. The modern youth set fire to the shop, and, the fire ends up engulfing the old woman because her leg was broken in the shuffle. The shrieks of the woman being burned alive make Alex want to vomit.
- To this, Dr. Brodsky says it's only his imagination. He won't be able to actually vomit, the doctor says.
- The fifth film Alex views takes place during World War Two. The Japanese soldiers in the film torture their captives by nailing them to trees, lighting them on fire, cutting off their testicles, and playing ball with their decapitated heads. Alex now feels such horrible pain in his head and belly that he screams for the film to be stopped.
- Dr. Brodsky laughs and reminds Alex that they've hardly started the treatment.

Part Two, Chapter Five

- Alex now refuses to describe the other films he has been forced to watch that afternoon, but he does let on that he believes Dr. Brodsky and Dr. Branom and all the white coats are sicker than any of the prisoners he's met. He simply could not think of any man sick enough to even think of making films of the kind he's being forced to watch.
- Finally, Alex is released – sick, tired and nauseous – back to his room. Dr. Branom comes in just as soon as Alex feels better after taking some milk and tea.
- Dr. Branom informs him of his positive progress, and warns him of two sessions to come – in the AM and PM – the next day.
- Callous and sympathetic at the same time, he says that the white coats have no choice but to be hard on Alex, since he must be cured.
- The two converse about how it is that Alex's body must be trained to become normal again and to unlearn evil by responding horribly to destruction.
- Alex realizes that the white coats must be doing something to make him ill, and he wonders if it's the wires that are attached to him.
- Dr. Branom pats Alex on the head and walks out.
- A Discharge Officer comes in to question Alex's plans upon release.
- When he regains his freedom, Alex plans on going home to surprise his parents, who have not been informed of his transfer and impending release in a fortnight.
- Some discussion takes place about the kinds of jobs a reformed criminal can have.
- Before exiting the room, the Discharge Officer challenges Alex to punch him in the face.
- Alex is puzzled, but attempts to punch the officer in the face anyhow.
- He immediately falls ill, thinking the whole incident rather funny.
- After dinner, Alex goes to sleep and has a nightmare about one of the films from that afternoon.
- At the height the dream about all the ultraviolence, he feels paralyzed and nauseated.
- He wakes up and attempts to get out of the room, only to find it locked and the windows barred. He realizes for the first time that there's no escaping from all of this.
- Worse, he doesn't dare to go back to sleep, not wanting to get sick.
- Soon enough, he manages to fall asleep anyhow and, thank goodness, he doesn't have to dream.

Part Two, Chapter Six

- This chapter opens with Alex screaming for the white coats to stop the film. He can't believe how torturous it is. Neither can we.
- Dr. Brodsky responds that Alex is doing really well; in fact, "first class."
- But it's the old Nazi film being shown again, accompanied by Ludwig van Beethoven's Fifth Symphony.
- Alex throws up while pleading with the white coats to stop the film and its musical accompaniment. He calls it a filthy unforgivable sin to play No. 5 while showing a Nazi film.
- Dr. Brodsky muses that he knows nothing about music himself, other than how it can be used as an emotional heightener.

- Dr. Branom calls it a necessary evil and the punishment "element" of the transformation technique that Alex is going through.
- Alex asks for a drink.
- Dr. Brodsky goes on to explain the classic conditioning and association treatment that he is being put through.
- Dr. Branom chimes in that it's like propaganda, or subliminal penetration.
- Alex wonders if it's the wires that are attached to him that make him ill.
- Dr. Brodsky denies this.
- It must be the needles, then, Alex reasons.
- Dr. Brodsky responds that it's no use objecting, because they could get this stuff of Ludovico's into his system in any way.
- Alex retreats, stating that he doesn't care about the ultraviolent films, but he won't forgive the white coats for playing Beethoven and Handel with the films.
- The white coats look a bit thoughtful before responding that it's just tough luck.
- Alex squirms, saying that he's learned his lesson and that his paradigm has been transformed. He's against violence, finally.
- The white coats state that there's no way he's cured yet, and definitely not until his body reacts automatically to violence – without further help, without the injection, and without the films, even.
- It doesn't matter, though, because only a little over a week remains of the treatment.
- The next day, Alex hits the nurse in order to avoid his shot.
- Unfortunately, this only results in four or five men in holding him down while another syringe gets jammed into his arm.
- Alex then skips the minutiae in his descriptions of the film-viewing. He states that the days seem to blend together as he's shown the same likeness of ultraviolent films: "Jap" torturers or Nazi shooters…whatever.
- Then, there comes a morning when he wakes up to have his breakfast and shot, and the nurse with the syringe never arrives.
- Today, Alex was going to walk to the screening room accompanied by a white coat.
- No syringes? None needed.
- The film rolls, and Alex feels sick. This time, though, he realizes that he can no longer blame the syringes for feeling sick and thirsty and full of aches. He realizes that the Ludovico stuff is like a vaccination, that his blood has been poisoned against the ultraviolence.
- Alex cries and cries and cries…
- That night, he lies in bed alone, contemplating escape.
- He fakes illness, crying out to the doctors that he is dying…
- White coats come running down the corridor to his rescue.
- Appendicitis! Pain! Appendicitis! (Seriously, that's what Alex screams.)
- A jangle of keys at the door. Alex prepares to throw his fists at the first fool that opens the locked door.
- Small problem: Alex envisions his unsuspecting victim in pain and a sickness arises in him as if it might kill him.
- Alex stumbles toward the bed in fear, moaning "urgh urgh urgh."
- The white coat witnesses what is happening and thinks it funny. He taunts Alex to a bit of a fist fight.
- Finally, while Alex lies there immobile, the white coat punches him in the face for his

deceit.

- Alex learns that he's become a total weakling, and that it now feels better to him to be hit than to throw a punch.
- In fact, had the white coat stayed, he might have turned the other cheek.

Part Two, Chapter Seven

- The fortnight is up for Alex; there's one real big day left; it's to be a "passing-out day." Whatever that means...we can only imagine.
- This morning, Alex is given the clothes he was wearing the night he was arrested, except now they're all nicely pressed. He's even given his knife back.
- Led quietly to the same old room, Alex notices that the curtains have been drawn in front of the silver screen, and the frosted viewing glass under the projection area has disappeared.
- The Staja Governor, the chaplain, the Minister of the Interior, the doctors and other white coats are all there.
- Dr. Brodsky welcomes everyone, introducing Alex as a "fit and well nourished" guy ready to be sent into the world again.
- "Actions speak louder than words...observe, all!"
- The lights go out. Two spotlights come on.
- One shines on Alex; the other – on a big dude he's never seen before.
- The man starts to insult Alex. Then he pinches Alex's nose, twists his ear... the pain stung.
- He challenges Alex to hit back.
- Alex reaches for his knife, and finds himself immediately overwhelmed by images of blood gushing out of this guy. He realizes that he has to change his own perception of his opponent before he starts to get sick.
- Alex pleads with the dude to take his cigarette, then his knife, then offers to clean his boots.
- Alex then licks his shoes. The audience roars with laughter.
- Just as the dude is about to hit Alex, Dr. Brodsky stops the madness.
- The dude bows and dances off like an actor. The lights come back on.
- Dr. Brodsky explains that Alex is not impelled towards the good by being impelled towards evil. Alex must not switch to a different attitude to battle the thoughts of evil that would make him sick. He goes on to say that Alex has no real choice, and the self-interest of avoiding physical pain drives him to become Jesus-like.
- Alex screeches, what about me? Am I just an animal? Am I just a clockwork orange? (Self-reference to the max. You go, Burgess!)
- Well, the chaplain says, this is the consequence of your evil choices. Too bad, boy.
- They call out a second actor, who's the most lovely young thing ever seen; Alex notes that she had real nice breasts.
- Aroused, Alex immediately thinks about raping her like a fierce savage.
- But a shot of sickness pierces through his daydream, and he knows he has to think about something else before it takes over completely.
- Alex breaks into what seems like a Shakespearean sonnet, offering to worship and protect the young actress.

- Let me be your true knight! (Seriously, now? Ludovico's Technique could make one into a romantic?)
- The actress smiles, bows, and dances off. The lights come back on. Applause.
- Dr. Brodsky announces that Alex will be a true Christian…ready to turn the other cheek, ready to be crucified rather than crucify, sick to the heart at the thought of even killing a fly.
- The Minister of the Interior starts to say how the Technique really works.
- The chaplain just says, "God help the lot of us."

Part Three, Chapter One

- What's it going to be then, eh?
- Standing outside of the white building the next day, Alex recounts his last day inside it.
- It tires him out, actually. He has to endure interviews for TV, photo sessions, demonstrations, and then, finally, a nap…Glad to put it all behind him.
- On an empty stomach, Alex decides to grab some grub. He witnesses the boorish men grab at a waitress who seems to enjoy the attention. He sits in dark corner to eat.
- A dwarf comes in to sell the morning paper. Alex purchases the paper – a Government publication – something about the upcoming General Election.
- It's so much propaganda from the boastful Government on the first page. Triumphs this, more police that.
- On the second page, he sees his own photograph: the first graduate from the State Institute for Reclamation of Criminal Types. Ludovico's Technique. A crime-free era coming up! The Minister of the Interior boasts about how clever the system is.
- Alex throws the paper on the floor in a fit of rage.
- A homebound Alex looks forward to surprising his parents, all the while dreaming about the classical music he'll be able to listen to in bed. Oh yeah, nothing like a little Mozart in bed.
- He takes the bus to Kingsley Avenue, and then to the flats of Flatblock 18A.
- It is quiet, since it is early winter morning.
- The apartment complex seems to him a bit cleaned up. The elevator even works.
- Alex opens the door to his home with the key he has in his pants, and is confronted by three pairs of frightened eyes.
- Mom and dad and some stranger stare back at him.
- The stranger is the first to ask him who the hell he is.
- Alex's parents start questioning how it was that he broke out of jail.
- Alex starts to explain, and the stranger starts to huff and puff…
- Alex questions him now: how long he's been there, what he does. He looks to be thirty or forty, very ugly, very middle-class.
- Alex's dad interrupts to defend the stranger, Joe. He lives there now; he's renting Alex's room.
- Joe speaks up and insults Alex, saying Alex has been a horrible son and that Joe's been protecting his parents like a son ought to.
- Well, this is funny, because Joe seems to Alex to be the same age as his parents.
- Upon seeing that his stereo and discs have gone missing from his room, Alex screams out in pain, calling Joe a horrible bastard.

- Alex's dad answers that all everything been taken away as compensation for the victims, a sort of new regulation by the State. After all, after their keeper died, the cats needed to be fed.
- A baffled Alex sits down.
- Joe demands that he ask permission before he sits.
- Alex retorts with profanity, and instantly feels pretty sick.
- The parents speak up. We can't just kick Joe out. He's supposed to be here for more time according to the rental agreement…
- Alex starts to cry, feeling very sorry for himself. His parents have gotten used to the peace and the extra rent money after two years…
- Well, his dad says, Joe's already paid the month's rent, so he can't go now.
- Joe cuts in and preaches just what a bad boy Alex has been and how he doesn't deserve kindness, nor parents, for that matter. Umm, AWKWARD!
- In tears, Alex speaks out about how everyone just wants him to suffer.
- Joe cuts in again, and says, basically, what goes around comes around.
- Alex staggers out of the door, saying that he'll never be seen again. And that he wishes he were back in prison.

Part Three, Chapter Two

- Alex wanders into the disc shop he used to frequent. It looks same-old, but without the old customer rep, Andy.
- Instead, some teenager mans the store now.
- Alex wants to listen to a bit of the Mozart Number Forty in the listening booth.
- The teenager makes fun of him.
- Alex feels his temper get hot, but quickly tries to forget about it, instead smiling at the flippant teenager.
- The music being piped over in the booth is not the Mozart Symphony Number Forty in G Minor, but the Mozart Prague. Usually, this would have enraged Alex, but before he can get angry, he feels sick to his stomach.
- He realizes he has forgotten how Ludovico's Technique has ruined all classical music for him.
- Crawling out of the booth sick and in pain, Alex staggers into the Korova Milkbar around the corner.
- The place is rather empty, since it is early morning. Alex orders some laced milk, size large.
- The hallucinogens work on Alex. He starts to trip on the whole world.
- He starts to make funny noises.
- He talks about God and his Angels and Saints…and sees them standing in front of him in a sea of statues.
- He feels light, almost like he's in Heaven.
- He grows warm and cold, and collapses…
- Alex starts to cry, feeling like death is the only answer to his sorrows.
- He doesn't know how he could kill himself without getting sick, though, as the thought of

himself bloodied by his own sword makes him sick.

- Alex walks to the public library to research other methods that enable him to die by drifting off into a dreamless sleep.
- This is an old public library, one that Alex could not recall going into since he was six-years-old.
- There are a lot of books, and Alex is bewildered, going from one to another.
- He flips through a medical book, but its descriptions and drawings of wounds and diseases only make him more sick.
- Then he takes down the Bible, thinking that it might give him comfort like the Staja days.
- Wrong; he starts to cry about Jews fighting with one another.
- An old man asks him what is the matter.
- The two converse.
- A second old man yells out that he recognizes Alex – the same man Alex and his entourage beat up two years ago in the alleyway!
- Alex responds that he's been punished for his crime since.
- Punishment? How about extermination, said the old man, whose name is Jack.
- Jack screams out for other ninety-year-olds to take hold of Alex so they can all teach him a lesson.
- They push and claw at Alex when a library attendant comes along.
- Alex pleads with the attendant to protect him, and to call the police.
- The old guys continue beating him up until the police arrive.

Part Three, Chapter Three

- The police have to beat up the old guys to disentangle Alex from them.
- OMG! The older cop is old Billyboy, Alex's enemy. And the younger one? None other than Dim, Alex's old droog-turned-traitor!
- Impossible, says Alex. He cannot believe that these modern youth are now all grown up and grown into cops – the dark side.
- Along with Rex (the third cop who's driving the patrol car), Billyboy and Dim force Alex into the backseat.
- Alex can't help but wonder whether it's all just a joke.
- Alex asks about Pete and says he feels sorry about Georgie. Dim teases Alex, pretending to forget who Pete is.
- They drive into the country.
- Alex freaks out. What's going on? He's been punished where punishment was due. He's been cured. Hasn't anyone read the papers?
- Dim punches Alex right in the nose. Blood drips out.
- They're in the country now, alright. Everything's quiet and barren.
- Rex sits at the wheel of the patrol car, smoking a cancer and reading a book while Billyboy and Dim do the unthinkable to Alex.
- Finally, the three cops drive away, leaving Alex lying there in the snow completely bloodied and disheveled.
- The rain starts. Alex gets up and begins walking.

Part Three, Chapter Four

- Alex stumbles upon a gate with HOME written on it. He swears he's seen this before.
- He knocks on the door, it opens.
- He tells the man he's been beaten up by the police and left to die on the road.
- The man leads Alex in to a warm fire.
- Alex knows right then what's so familiar about HOME.
- The man, who is middle-aged, offers Alex some whiskey for warming up.
- On the table rests a typewriter and a bunch of papers. Alex recalls the manuscript, *A Clockwork Orange*, that he had torn up in a past life.
- The writer makes Alex a nice bath and offers him a full supper.
- Alex swells up with tears.
- Alex bathes, gets in some pajamas already laid out for him, and has supper with the writer.
- He speaks of repayment.
- The writer interrupts him, stating that he knows who he is. Suspense!
- He's seen Alex's picture in the papers earlier this morning. Yes! It's Alex, alright.
- The man tries to give Alex his sympathies in his struggle against the government and the police.
- The man urges Alex to tell his story.
- Alex treads carefully, giving little detail about his crimes.
- But he does not hold back on the juicy bits about Ludovico's Technique.
- The writer is enraged about it! Cruel and unusual punishment, he cries. Alex is no longer a human being, lacking the power of choice, he utters. Could Burgess have chosen a more convenient mouthpiece?
- The writer wants Alex to help dislodge the current overbearing Government, one that is content to turn a decent person into a piece of repressed clockwork.
- Alex agrees with the writer, but seems to be more concerned with how fervently he's been wiping the same dinner plate.
- The writer launches into a huge speech about how ever since his wife has gone, he's been having a hard time doing the chores around the house by himself.
- He goes into detail about his wife's rape and murder.
- Alex recalls the vivid details of that unfortunate night he participated in. He starts to get sick.
- The writer orders Alex to bed.

Part Three, Chapter Five

- After a really nice night's sleep, Alex walks around in the room trying to figure out the writer's name.
- He has the fantastic idea of looking for the writer's name on a manuscript of *A Clockwork Orange*.
- It turns out to be F. Alexander. Great. Another Alex.

- He leafs through the book, wondering if F. Alexander has gone crazy because of his wife's death.
- F. Alexander calls him from downstairs and hands him some boiled eggs and black toast.
- He informs Alex that he's been making phone calls all morning to people who might be interested in his case, him being a "very potent weapon" against the Government in this sensitive time just before the election.
- He characterizes the Government as a brutal totalitarian regime.
- Alex wonders out loud why F. Alexander is so hot and strong against the Government.
- The thoughtful writer says that he's defending liberty, or at least the tradition of it. Whatever that means.
- And what does Alex get out of this, he wonders? Can he return to his enjoyment of classical music?
- Well, F. Alexander ducks the question, and instead shows Alex an article he's written for him, soon to be published in *The Weekly Trumpet*.
- It was a long, weepy piece, but Alex is kind enough to call it "real horrorshow" to F. Alexander.
- Come again?
- Horrorshow is nadsat speak for all modern youth, Alex explains. F. Alexander hurries off to do the dishes.
- The doorbell rings. Three men, Z. Dolin, Rubinstein, and D. B. da Silva stand there looking at Alex.
- The four of them converse.
- F. Alexander becomes suspicious because Alex's speech reminds him of someone else's speech pattern in a former life…uh, oh!
- Alex starts to argue with the three folks, but primarily Z. Dolin, who apparently wants him to be a martyr to the cause of liberty.
- Alex objects, crying that he doesn't want to be a plaything, an idiot that anyone could just use. After all, he's not dim.
- Dim? F. Alexander raises an eyebrow.
- What's Dim got to do with it? Alex retorts, without thinking.
- F. Alexander goes mad, shouting out loud that if this were the same coincidence that raped and killed his wife he'd tear Alex up and split him apart real good.
- D. B. da Silva tries to calm F. Alexander down.
- Alex tries to leave.
- Z. Dolin grabs a hold of him.
- F. Alexander looks like a lunatic at this point, and keeps chanting Dim… dim dim dim.
- Alex is dragged into town by F. Alexander's associates.
- They arrive at an apartment, plop Alex in, and tells him that this is his new home.
- Before they leave, however, they ask Alex whether he's the person F. Alexander feared.
- Alex responds that he's paid for his sins.
- The associates leave to go about their political business. Alex is left feeling a bit sick with the thought of his previous crime and lies down to sleep.
- When he wakes up, he hears Symphony Number Three of the Danish composer, Otto Skadelig, through the wall. A particularly somber and violent piece.
- For two seconds, Alex manages to enjoy it; until, of course, the pain and sickness overcome him.
- He bangs on the wall for it to be turned off.

- He crashes against the wall until his knuckles bleed.
- He plugs his ears with his fingers – no luck!
- He bangs against the door – it is locked!
- He looks at the pamphlet that lies on the table in his room, but it reads only DEATH TO THE GOVERNMENT. He sees another that reads, "Open the window to fresh air, fresh ideas, a new way of living."
- From these, he knows what he has to do.
- As he leaps from the window several stories above ground, he bids farewell to the world, "May God forgive you for a ruined life."

Part Three, Chapter Six

- Alex jumps and falls hard on the sidewalk.
- Broken back, broken wrists, broken bones…
- Before he passes out, it becomes clear to him that F. Alexander and his associates are trying to force his suicide to suit their own political agenda against the Government.
- After a long, black gap of perhaps a million years in the hospital, Alex comes to not knowing who he is or why he's totally bandaged up. He can't feel anything.
- The nurse hails white coats, who arrive with the prison chaplain; he tells Alex that he's quit the Staja and is now doing sermons.
- Alex drifts in and out of consciousness for a while.
- He comes to with Z. Dolin, Rubinstein, and D. B. da Silva there, calling him "friend" and saying how well he has served "Liberty."
- Alex protests this, but it doesn't work because his mouth is bandaged up.
- F. Alexander's entourage shows Alex various headlines from the papers bearing a "Down with the Government" message. This excites Alex (in a bad way), and the nurse has to shoo out the entourage.
- Alex falls into a dream, during which he's doing ultraviolent stuff like in the olden days. A little bit of smashing into a parked auto, a bit of raping young girls, this and that.
- He wakes up to find his parents by his bed. His father tells him that Joe has left the flat, and that Alex should come home. His mother just sobs.
- Alex orders them out of his room with a lot of violent profanity.
- He realizes that he can think violent thoughts and not get sick.
- He asks the nurse how long he's been there.
- A week or so.
- Alex asks her to confirm that Ludovico's Technique has been reversed.
- She says it's all for the best.
- A couple of days later, a pair of doctors ask him a series of inane questions using picture books (of stupid things like eggs and peacocks) and what not. They further confirm for Alex that he's been cured of Ludovico's Technique by doctors who used "deep hypnopaedia" on him. (We think that means hypnosis.)
- More time passes and Alex gets a lot better. At 2:30pm one day, he receives a special visit from the Minister of the Interior, dressed in the heighth of fashion, of course, and followed by a dozen of journalists and photographers.

- The minister calls Alex a friend, but Alex calls him an enemy.
- The two converse cryptically for a while.
- The Minister now tells Alex that he's been cured, after all, and that a high-paying job is lined up for him when he checks out. He also reminds Alex that it was the Government that ultimately put away the crazy lunatic, F. Alexander, that wants his life.
- Distracted by the thought, a photographer screams out, SMILE! and Alex complies.
- A picture of the two looking like old friends is taken.
- Now, the Minister brings in a present – a stereo!
- Beethoven's Ninth is just a signature away, they tell him.
- Alex signs, and the symphony that ensues is glorious.

Part Three, Chapter Seven

- What's it going to be then, eh? Of course this ends the chapter, and Part Three, and the book. Did you see it coming? We sure did.
- There's Alex, and his three new friends – Len, Rick, and Bully.
- The four of them sit in the Korova Milkbar drinking some milk-plus and trying to figure out what trouble to get into.
- They are still dressed in the heighth of fashion, which has changed a bit these days from really tight to very loose. Apparently, they have also shaved their heads, because it this is totally in nowadays.
- Alex, the oldest of the four, is the natural leader. However, he's gotten the idea of late that Bully wants to take over. But, whatever, Alex is with bored being the leader anyway.
- After all, he has the best (paying) job of the four, being in the National Gramodisc Archives on the music side.
- Randomly, but presumably feeling the drugs kick in, Alex punches some dude in the stomach and orders his friends out of the bar.
- Bully makes it an unlucky day for an old guy he punches.
- The boys suggest getting a glass of something hot at the Duke of New York, not far away.
- Alex grants permission, and he and his entourage slip into the bar, where they sit down next to the same old women we saw at the opening of the book.
- They flirt with Alex for a round of freebies.
- Alex isn't feeling it, saying that his cash is hard-earned.
- Seeing the eagerness of the old women, though, he loosens up and orders them a round. He orders a small beer for himself.
- As he pulls the money out of his pockets, a newspaper clipping of a baby drops to the floor. His entourage makes fun of him.
- Alex tears up the photo, embarrassed.
- Still not feeling it, Alex excuses himself and suggests meeting the next night.
- It is dark outside, and Alex is feeling just as somber. He notes that lately his down moods have been dictating what music he listens to. Instead of great, violent symphonies, he's more partial to sappy romantic songs. What the heck?!
- He walks into a coffeehouse for a cup of tea.
- Sitting by himself for a while, he realizes that his old droog Pete is there with his wife,

Georgina.

- Apparently, Pete married at nineteen and is now part of the working class, sporting a moustache and an ordinary day-suit.
- The two update each other about Georgie and Dim.
- Georgina is amused by Alex's funny speech.
- Pete reveals that he is working hard at the State Marine Insurance office and that Georgina is a typist. The two manage to get by in a small flat.
- Alex cannot believe how grown up Pete seems…and married, too!
- The two of them seem very much in love.
- The couple leaves Alex.
- Alex continues to sit in the coffeehouse, thinking about how time has passed him by. After all, he's eighteen now, and eighteen is not such a young age anymore. At eighteen, Mozart had written concertos, symphonies, and operas. Mendelssohn had composed his greatest overture… What's it going to be for not-so-little Alex?
- Back out in the dark winter streets, Alex envisions his adulthood. He likes the idea of a wife, a mother to his son.
- A son to whom he would teach what life has taught him. Of course, the little poophead wouldn't listen to him, but that's just how it's supposed to be.
- A youth has to grow up on its own terms.
- Anyway, a wife and a son: that was something new to do, like a new chapter in a book, this book of life.

Themes

Theme of Fate and Free Will

A Clockwork Orange highlights the question of whether people are destined to their fate, or whether free will and external circumstances can influence people's life outcomes. Alex believes that humans are born evil and need cultivation to avoid evil. F. Alexander believes that humans are born good, but are corrupted by society and culture. The Government believes that the stability of the State trumps the happiness of its citizens, and readily abolishes moral choice (a fundamental human trait) in the name of stability. In contrast to this, Alex fights vehemently against the notion that his freedom to choose should be compromised at all, as free will is what makes him human to begin with.

Questions About Fate and Free Will

1. Do you believe that humans are born and destined to be evil, needing cultivation and societal pressures to become good? Or do you believe that we are basically born good, but are corrupted by our social environment? Justify your position with examples from the book.
2. What are some fundamental characteristics of human beings? That is, what makes us different from machines, robots, or other animals? Do the characters in this book possess some of these traits?

3. In what sense is evil part of Alex's nature and fate? Is the ability to perform evil deeds, freely and openly, an important part of being human?

Chew on Fate and Free Will

A central part of being human is free will, the ability to choose among different options. While Alex has freedom of choice, he is as human as possible. When Alex is rendered unable to choose violence, thanks to Ludovico's Technique, Burgess sends the message that he no longer is human, but a mere clockwork orange.

People are born innocent, only to be corrupted by society and its ills. Societal corruption, though, is neither necessary nor irreversible. Alex, the protagonist-narrator of *A Clockwork Orange*, is the perfect case in point.

Theme of Morality and Ethics

The central message of this book seems to be that the freedom to choose (good or evil) is fundamental to mankind. Indeed, this element of moral choice distinguishes humans from machines and robots. However, is moral depravity better than forced morality? Are evil and suffering (freely chosen and caused by people) better than a docile, peaceful state (engineered by the Government)? People like Alex, the prison chaplain, and F. Alexander and co. seem to think so. The State is more interested in stability than any debate on morality and ethics, however.

Questions About Morality and Ethics

1. Which is a more moral person: a kid who consistently but freely chooses to do evil deeds over good ones or a reformed criminal who has been brainwashed to choose only good deeds? Be ready to explain your reasoning and assumptions.
2. Is moral depravity better than forced morality? Where does amorality figure in all of this? Which side of the debate does each major character in this book take?
3. Do you believe in the adage, "what goes around comes around"? Does Alex get what is due to him?
4. Do you consider F. Alexander to be a morally upright man? How about the Minister of the Interior – are his actions morally justified?

Chew on Morality and Ethics

Behavior that is not chosen, but dictated or forced, is neither moral nor immoral, because the freedom to choose one's actions underlies the very concept of "morality."

Alex is the ultimate poster-child for amorality, since he delights in violence for violence's sake.

Theme of Manipulation

The Government in Alex's world is rather Machiavellian, and will do anything to ensure its own survival as well as the stability of the State. To that end, it does not blink twice employing questionable scientific techniques to manipulate its citizens into becoming moral exemplars. The manipulation technique used on Alex is called Ludovico's Technique, or basically, behavioral modification through associative learning.

Questions About Manipulation

1. How many different kinds of manipulation can you name? In how many different ways does the Government manipulate its citizens in Alex's world? Through what means? For what purpose?
2. What, in your view, is behavior modification? How is it done? Why is it done? How is it different from bribery, for example?
3. Can advertising be seen as manipulation and as a behavior modification tool? Does the fact that advertising can cause behavioral changes bother you?
4. Do you possess vices for which you wish you could undergo Ludovico's Technique? Would you do so if offered the chance?

Chew on Manipulation

Forcing Alex to undergo the Reclamation Treatment is just one out of the many ways the Government manipulates its citizens to ensure stability in the State.

Alex is forced to endure Ludovico's Technique, which employs the principles of associative learning, whereby a person's behavior is modified through prolonged manipulation of her normal responses to select stimuli. In this day and age, Ludovico's Technique would be considered torture, or at least the unethical treatment of criminals.

Theme of Good vs. Evil

The battle between good and evil gets complicated in *A Clockwork Orange*, because the novel really presents the battle between *forced* good and *chosen* evil. Who is better: someone incapable of doing evil, only good, or someone with the freedom to choose whatever path she wants, but opts do evil? Is a "clockwork Christian" more interesting than the likes of Alex? Or is evil Alex more human than the clockwork doer of good deeds? We know this at least: Burgess sides with Alex.

Questions About Good vs. Evil

1. What are your thoughts on the following quote, which the prison chaplain says to Alex? "The question is whether such a technique can really make a man good. Goodness comes from within...

Chew on Good vs. Evil

The prison chaplain says that personal choice is required for a person to be deemed "good." Per this view, a religious person who does not thoughtfully choose her actions, but blindly follows the words of her religion's instructions to do only good deeds cannot be seen as a "good" person.

Despite all the talk surrounding the good vs. evil debate in *A Clockwork Orange*, Burgess has included precious few instances of true, freely chosen goodness in the book.

Theme of Power

In *A Clockwork Orange*, the Government seeks to suppress individuals and individual choice in favor of the stability of the State, largely to ensure its own survival. Towards this end, the Government is prepared to do anything necessary, including distributing propaganda and censorship, employing morally questionable scientific techniques to "reform" criminals, and employing criminals as state patrol to threaten other citizens (and potential political dissidents).

Questions About Power

1. In what ways does the Government seek to control its citizens? Is it primarily physical, psychological, or emotional suppression?
2. Why does the Government decrease the number of street patrol cars at night, when, arguably, the town most needs them? What ulterior motive must the Government have in choosing to do this?
3. How does a majority culture of violent teens reflect upon its Government?
4. Give specific examples of how the Government changes its policy against criminals from part one to part three of the book.

Chew on Power

From its treatment of Alex, one can clearly gauge how the Government is willing to sacrifice the individual liberties of its constituents for the stability of the State.

The Government is the chief antagonistic force against Alex in *A Clockwork Orange*, because of the differing views it espouses on the subjects of morality, personal liberty, and freedom of choice.

Theme of Transformation

Burgess values transformation a decent amount, and has famously said that a book without a hint of "moral progress" or personal transformation has no point and is better left unwritten. Thus, despite all the crime Alex commits, at the end of the day, he grows up. The transformation Alex experiences in the novel is hard-earned and long overdue; it is also freely chosen and deeply personal for him.

Questions About Transformation

1. In what ways does Alex undergo personal and moral transformation from the beginning to the end of the book? How can you tell? Does the transformation manifest itself through his actions, or just his thoughts?
2. Does Alex's transformation seem sudden or surprising to you? Is it fitting? Natural? Could *A Clockwork Orange* have done without the last chapter?
3. Who and what are chiefly responsible for causing Alex to suddenly grow up? In what ways is his maturation like a religious awakening? In what senses is it hard-earned and long in coming?
4. How does F. Alexander transform from part one to part three?

Chew on Transformation

Alex's "transformation" in the last chapter is completely superficial and will not last, for he has come by it due to boredom with his current life and out of envy for Pete's "normal" life.

The transformation F. Alexander has experienced might more appropriately be called degeneration. He goes from being an aspiring writer who loves his wife to a vengeful political dissident.

Theme of Violence

Violence and instances of criminality are ubiquitous in this book. In just a few chapters, Alex and his entourage have performed every trick in the criminal's Bible: boozing, doing drugs, mugging, robbing, gang fighting, grand theft auto, gang rape, reckless driving, vandalism, arson, and murder. What is more, there's also plenty of discussion of probation officers, juvenile delinquents, prison life, police brutality, and even a forced suicide.

Questions About Violence

1. Of all the acts of violence Alex and his gang perpetrate on their victims, which is/are the worst? What criteria do you use to assess this, the amount of perceived pain (whether it results in death or not), or something else?
2. What role does violence or criminality play in this novel? Could the book have done without all that brutality?
3. Alex commits crimes for the sheer joy of it. Do you think Dim and Georgie operate similarly? What motivates Dim to act violently? What motivates Georgie? Are either of them any different from Alex?
4. How do you suppose the "modern youth" have become so violent? Is it due to lack of parenting, authority, sense of morality, or something else?

Chew on Violence

Alex commits crimes for the sheer joy of it; Dim is too dim to be thoughtful about his motivations; and Georgie commits crimes for monetary gain. Thus, Alex and Georgie are your typical criminals, while Dim is a mere victim of his circumstances.

In his vivid descriptions of brutality in the work, Burgess uses violence not only to contrast the forces of good and evil, but also to cause readers to look within themselves at their own capacities for nastiness. Thus, the depictions of violence are indispensable to *A Clockwork Orange*.

Theme of Language and Communication

Language, specifically nadsat, has an important several important functions in this work. First, it works as a literary device that seeks to temporarily alienate the reader from the world of the protagonist-narrator. We are initially barred from making moral judgments of Alex and co. because we aren't sure of what they are doing; we are shielded and removed from some of Alex's brutality against others. As we toil for the first several chapters learning to decipher the language, however, we build rapport with the violent teens, and even fancy that we understand them (because we have learned their language). Second, since nadsat draws its inspirations from Russian and Cockney English, it tells us about the author's political message. In Burgess's time, Russian was a seriously repressed totalitarian state, and Alex's fictional British world is not much different. Third, as we discuss in the "Characterization" section, an individual's use of language tells us a good deal about his place, function, and role in society.

Questions About Language and Communication

1. By what chapter did you finally catch on to nadsat? Can you understand it now with relative ease? Did you notice a shift in your attitude towards Alex and/or towards his conduct once you clued into exactly what he was saying and doing?
2. Did you find yourself liking Alex more or less before or after you were able to decipher nadsat for yourself?
3. What roles does a made-up language like nadsat play in a violent novel like this one?
4. Could *A Clockwork Orange* been as effective a book had it been written without nadsat? Why or why not?

Chew on Language and Communication

The origins of nadsat betray the political message Burgess intends to convey through its usage – that Alex's Britain is not that far off from being a totalitarian state like Russia.

Nadsat is indispensable to *A Clockwork Orange* as a literary device. Without it, readers would never have the opportunity to develop the requisite rapport with the protagonist to stick with him through the end.

Quotes

Fate and Free Will Quotes

But, brothers, this biting of their toe-nails over what is the cause of badness is what turns me into a fine laughing malchick. They don't go into the cause of goodness, so why the other shop? If lewdies are good that's because they like it, and I wouldn't ever interfere with their pleasures, and so of the other shop. And I was patronizing the other shop. More, badness is of the self, the one, the you or me on our oddy knockies, and that self is made by old Bog or God and is his great pride and radosty. But the not-self cannot have the bad, meaning they of the government and the judges and the schools cannot allow the bad because they cannot allow the self. And is not our modern history, my brothers, the story of brave malenky selves fighting these big machines? I am serious with you, brothers, over this. But what I do I do because I like to do. (1.4.21)

Thought: To Alex, just as goodness can be natural or inherent to some people, so can badness. People can be born good or bad – either way it is natural. To come up with a causal explanation for certain characteristics is nonsensical, at least to Alex. A Clockwork Orange seems to argue that what is most important is having the free will to choose to act accordingly to one's inherent nature.

"Very hard ethical questions are involved," he went on. "You are to be made into a good boy, 6655321. Never again will you have the desire to commit acts of violence or to offend in any way whatsoever against the State's Peace. I hope you take all that in. I hope you are absolutely clear in your own mind about that." (2.3.11)

Thought: The prison chaplain cautions Alex about how his fundamental nature will be changed by enrolling in the Reclamation Treatment program. Specifically, his desire to be violent will be abolished altogether, and he will not have the free will to choose actions that spring from a violent nature.

"It may not be nice to be good, little 6655321. It may be horrible to be good. And when I say that to you I realize how self-contradictory that sounds. I know I shall have many sleepless nights about this. What does God want? Does God want goodness or the choice of goodness? Is a man who chooses the bad perhaps in some ways better than a man who has the good imposed upon him? Deep and hard questions..." (2.3.13)

Thought: The prison chaplain suggests to Alex that he might not enjoy losing his free will and being forced to be "good." Are we supposed to be what we are supposed to be? That is the real question.

"Life is a very wonderful thing," said Dr. Branom in a like very holy goloss. "The processes of life, the make-up of the human organism, who can fully understand these miracles? Dr. Brodsky is, of course, a remarkable man. What is happening to you now is what should happen to any normal healthy human organism contemplating the actions of the forces of evil, the workings of the principle of destruction. You are being made sane, you are being made healthy." (2.5.9)

Thought: Interestingly, Dr. Brodsky believes that Ludovico's Technique is restoring "human nature" to Alex, rather than taking it away from him. Even if it means the removal of Alex's free will, Dr. Brodsky believes in forcing people to conform to a "norm" of human instincts and behavior.

"You felt ill this afternoon," he said, "because you're getting better. When we're healthy we respond to the presence of the hateful with fear and nausea. You're becoming healthy, that's all. You'll be healthier still this time tomorrow." (2.5.13)

Thought: It is noteworthy that Dr. Brodsky treats Alex as sick, needing to be made healthy in order to act normally or "humanly" towards violence and crime. This "healing" also removes Alex's ability to act freely.

I thought to myself, "Hell hell hell, there might be a chance for me if I get out now." (2.6.34)

Thought: Towards the end of Alex's treatment, he contemplates escape, because he does not want to be transformed into a clockwork orange, a nonhuman, an automaton without moral choice and free will.

And what, brothers, I had to escape into sleep from then was the horrible and wrong feeling that it was better to get the hit than give it. If that veck had stayed I might even have like presented the other cheek. (2.6.39)

Thought: To Alex, it is not natural for a person to do what Jesus Christ advises – to "turn the other cheek" when attacked. In this situation, Alex laments that he might have been conditioned (forced) to act upon this advice against his free will.

Dr. Brodsky said to the audience: "Our subject is, you see, impelled towards the good by, paradoxically, being impelled towards evil. The intention to act violently is accompanied by strong feelings of physical distress. To counter these the subject has to switch to a diametrically opposed attitude. Any questions?" (2.7.12)

Thought: How does Dr. Brodsky convince himself that it is natural for humans to choose to be nonviolent in order to avoid getting sick by thinking violent thoughts? How can it be natural if your acts are dictated by fear or avoidance behavior and not by free will?

"Choice," rumbled a rich deep goloss. I viddied it belonged to the prison charlie. "He has no real choice, has he? Self-interest, fear of physical pain, drove him to that grotesque act of self-abasement. Its insincerity was clearly to be seen. He ceases to be a wrongdoer. He ceases also to be a creature capable of moral choice." (2.7.13)

Thought: In other words, if Alex ceases to be a wrongdoer only because he is afraid of physical pain, he ceases to be human or, by extension, a creature capable of making moral choices or using his free will.

"They have turned you into something other than a human being. You have no power of choice any longer. You are committed to socially acceptable acts, a little machine capable only of good. And I see that clearly--that business about the marginal conditionings. Music and the sexual act, literature and art, all must be a source now not of pleasure but of pain." (3.4.17)

Thought: F. Alexander verbalizes a key point of A Clockwork Orange. Robbed of his free will and choice to do good or evil things, and compelled to perform only socially acceptable acts, Alex is no longer a human being.

"A man who cannot choose ceases to be a man." (3.4.19)

Thought: This may be the most lucid statement of what a clockwork orange represents. The moral of the story? If you have no free will and can't choose, you're not human. Likewise, if you can't choose, you can't be good or evil, because it no longer makes sense to talk about actions as good or evil.

Morality and Ethics Quotes

"Very hard ethical questions are involved," he went on. "You are to be made into a good boy, 6655321. Never again will you have the desire to commit acts of violence or to offend in any way whatsoever against the State's Peace. I hope you take all that in. I hope you are absolutely clear in your own mind about that." (2.3.11)

Thought: The prison chaplain cautions Alex that by enrolling in the treatment program, his desire to do evil will be abolished altogether. Indeed, he will be forced to do good and to not offend. He will no longer have a moral choice. Does he really want this? The chaplain acknowledges how hard an ethical question this is.

"It may not be nice to be good, little 6655321. It may be horrible to be good. And when I say that to you I realize how self-contradictory that sounds. I know I shall have many sleepless nights about this. What does God want? Does God want goodness or the choice of goodness? Is a man who chooses the bad perhaps in some ways better than a man who has the good imposed upon him? Deep and hard questions…" (2.3.13)

Thought: The prison chaplain suggests to Alex that he might not enjoy being forced to be "good." That is to say, he might get more enjoyment out of having a moral choice. Then the chaplain zooms out and ponders what God intends for all of us. Does He want us only to do good? Or has He intended that we choose as we please and live with our decisions?

"But, sir, sirs, I see that it's wrong. It's wrong because it's against like society, it's wrong because every veck on earth has the right to live and be happy without being beaten and tolchocked and knifed. I've learned a lot, oh really I have." (2.6.22-23)

Thought: Alex pretends to have access to a moral system in order to avoid not being able to enjoy classical music ever again. This suggests to us that Alex has really possessed systems of morality and ethics from the get-go.

"The heresy of an age of reason," or some such slovos. "I see what is right and approve, but I do what is wrong. No, no, my boy, you must leave it all to us. But be cheerful about it. It will soon be all over. In less than a fortnight now you'll be a free man." Then he patted me on the pletcho. (2.2.24)

Thought: The doctor thinks Alex's system of morality is all out of whack: he sees what is right, but he still chooses to behave badly. To the doctor, consistency in thought and action (as in, what *should* one do given one's circumstances) is the most important factor in morality.

And what, brothers, I had to escape into sleep from then was the horrible and wrong feeling that it was better to get the hit than give it. If that veck had stayed I might even have like presented the other cheek. (2.6.39)

Thought: Isn't it interesting that Alex believes that it is "horrible and wrong" to do the Christian thing by turning the other cheek? What does this say about his system of morality? Is it warped?

Dr. Brodsky said to the audience: "Our subject is, you see, impelled towards the good by, paradoxically, being impelled towards evil. The intention to act violently is accompanied by strong feelings of physical distress. To counter these the subject has to switch to a diametrically opposed attitude. Any questions?" (2.7.12)

Thought: Can we speak of morality when a person, by being impelled towards the good, actually ends up being inclined towards evil? If you're skirting your intentions due to physical distress, are you acting in accordance with your morality or simply out of physical compulsion?

"Choice," rumbled a rich deep goloss. I viddied it belonged to the prison charlie. "He has no real choice, has he? Self-interest, fear of physical pain, drove him to that grotesque act of self-abasement. Its insincerity was clearly to be seen. He ceases to be a wrongdoer. He ceases also to be a creature capable of moral choice."

"These are subtleties," like smiled Dr. Brodsky. "We are not concerned with motive, with the higher ethics. We are concerned only with cutting down crime--" (2.7.13-14)

Thought: The Government is not concerned with the higher, philosophical questions of ethics and choice.

"You are passing now to a region where you will be beyond the reach of the power of prayer. A terrible terrible thing to consider. And yet, in a sense, in choosing to be deprive of the ability to make an ethical choice, you have in a sense really chosen the good. So I shall like to think. So, God help us all…" (2.3.13)

Thought: The chaplain laments that Alex has reached a point at which he can no longer make an ethical choice between good and evil. This makes him essentially non-human, and God can't possibly affect that.

Manipulation Quotes

I had to have a smeck, though, thinking of what I'd viddied once in one of these like articles on Modern Youth, about how Modern Youth would be better off if A Lively Appreciation Of The Arts could be like encouraged. Great Music, it said, and Great Poetry would like quieted Modern Youth down and make Modern Youth more Civilized. Civilized my syphilised yarbles. Music always sort of sharpened me up, O my brothers, and made me feel like old Bog himself, ready to make with the old donner and blitzen and have vecks and ptitsas creeching away in my ha ha power. (1.4.24)

Thought: Interesting thought: education and appreciation for the arts and music can manipulate shy little rascals into becoming high-achieving kids. Alex bastardizes this idea, though, because he admittedly uses the power of music to be even more violent towards others.

"Common criminals like this unsavoury crowd"--(that meant me, brothers, as well as the others, who were real prestoopnicks and treacherous with it)--"can best be dealt with on a purely curative basis. Kill the criminal reflex, that's all. Full implementation in a year's time. Punishment means nothing to them, you can see that. They enjoy their so-called punishment. They start murdering each other." (2.2.17)

Thought: This "curative" approach sounds great in theory, but doesn't it strike you as a bit inhumane? But then, all sorts of manipulation can sound morally questionable. And then you get stuck with the question: how can one reform criminals at all?

"You had a very positive response. Tomorrow, of course, there'll be two sessions, morning and afternoon, and I should imagine that you'll be feeling a bit limp at the end of the day. But we have to be hard on you, you have to be cured." (2.5.5)

Thought: The behavior modification sessions are tough on Alex. They are supposed to cure him of his tendencies to do evil, though, so of course the Government thinks it's a fair trade-off. He's already sinned, so now it should be a prize for him to be reformed.

"You felt ill this afternoon," he said, "because you're getting better. When we're healthy we respond to the presence of the hateful with fear and nausea. You're becoming healthy, that's all. You'll be healthier still this time tomorrow." (2.5.13)

Thought: Ironically, by getting sick, Alex becomes healthier once the manipulation treatment is underway.

"Right," said Dr. Brodsky. "It's association, the oldest educational method in the world. And what really causes you to feel ill." (2.6.12)

Thought: So, it is finally revealed to us in plain English that the manipulation/behavior modification treatment Alex is undergoing employs the oldest educational method in the world – associative learning.

Now I knew that I'd have to be real skorry and get my cut-throat britva out before this horrible killing sickness whooshed up and turned the like joy of battle into feeling I was going to snuff it. But, O brothers, as my rooker reached for the britva in my inside carman I got this like picture in my mind's glazzy of this insulting chelloveck howling for mercy with the red red krovvy all streaming out of his rot, and hot after this picture the sickness and dryness and pains were rushing to overtake, and I viddied that I'd have to change the way I felt about this rotten veck very very skorry indeed… (2.7.6)

Thought: This is the first sign that Ludovico's Technique works. Alex's behavior has definitely changed.

Dr. Brodsky said to the audience: "Our subject is, you see, impelled towards the good by, paradoxically, being impelled towards evil. The intention to act violently is accompanied by strong feelings of physical distress. To counter these the subject has to switch to a diametrically opposed attitude. Any questions?" (2.7.12)

Thought: Here, Dr. Brodsky is explaining the mechanism for behavior modification/manipulation. But how in the world does Dr. Brodsky convince himself that it is natural for humans to choose to be nonviolent in order to avoid getting sick by thinking violent thoughts? How is that human? How can it be natural if your acts are dictated by fear or avoidance behavior?

Good vs. Evil Quotes

But, brothers, this biting of their toe-nails over what is the cause of badness is what turns me into a fine laughing malchick. They don't go into the cause of goodness, so why the other shop? If lewdies are good that's because they like it, and I wouldn't ever interfere with their pleasures, and so of the other shop. And I was patronizing the other shop. More, badness is of the self, the one, the you or me on our oddy knockies, and that self is made by old Bog or God and is his great pride and radosty. But the not-self cannot have the bad, meaning they of the government and the judges and the schools cannot allow the bad because they cannot allow the self. And is not our modern history, my brothers, the story of brave malenky selves fighting these big machines? I am serious with you, brothers, over this. But what I do I do because I like to do. (1.4.21)

Thought: To Alex, just as goodness can be natural or inherent to some people, so can badness. People can be born good or bad – either way it is natural. To come up with a causal explanation for certain characteristics is nonsensical, at least to Alex.

"It may not be nice to be good, little 6655321. It may be horrible to be good. And when I say that to you I realize how self-contradictory that sounds. I know I shall have many sleepless nights about this. What does God want? Does God want goodness or the choice of goodness? Is a man who chooses the bad perhaps in some ways better than a man who has the good imposed upon him? Deep and hard questions…" (2.3.13)

Thought: The prison chaplain suggests to Alex that he might not enjoy being forced to be "good." Are we supposed to be what we are supposed to be? That is the real question.

"You are passing now to a region where you will be beyond the reach of the power of prayer. A terrible terrible thing to consider. And yet, in a sense, in choosing to be deprive of the ability to make an ethical choice, you have in a sense really chosen the good. So I shall like to think. So, God help us all…" (2.3.13)

Thought: The chaplain laments that Alex has reached a point where he can no longer make an ethical choice between good and evil. This makes him essentially non-human, and God can't possibly affect him any more.

Power Quotes

He just sort of looked right through us poor plennies, saying, in a very beautiful real educated goloss: "The Government cannot be concerned any longer with outmoded penological theories. Cram criminals together and see what happens. You get concentrated criminality, crime in the midst of punishment. Soon we may be needing all our prison space for political offenders." (2.2.17)

Thought: Forget the criminals, we need the space for political dissidents! These are the true colors of the Government. Aside from not caring about individual criminals, the Government seeks to free up space for the forces of subversion it seems to have imprisoned. What better way to quell discontent than to jail all dissidents.

"Choice," rumbled a rich deep goloss. I viddied it belonged to the prison charlie. "He has no real choice, has he? Self-interest, fear of physical pain, drove him to that grotesque act of self-abasement. Its insincerity was clearly to be seen. He ceases to be a wrongdoer. He ceases also to be a creature capable of moral choice."

"These are subtleties," like smiled Dr. Brodsky. "We are not concerned with motive, with the higher ethics. We are concerned only with cutting down crime--" (2.7.13-14)

Thought: The Government is not concerned with individual motives, nor with the higher, philosophical questions of ethics and choice. Indeed, the Government cares more about crime control and really doesn't want anything to do with the individual.

"The point is," this Minister of the Inferior was saying real gromky, "that it works." (2.7.25)

Thought: The Minister of the Interior embodies the pragmatic, Machiavellian attitude of the Government: as long as IT WORKS, anyone can be sacrificed.

What it said underneath my picture was that here was the first graduate from the new State Institute for Reclamation of Criminal Types, cured of his criminal instincts in a fortnight only, now a good law-fearing citizen and all that cal. Then I viddied there was a very boastful article about this Ludovico's Technique and how clever the Government was and all that cal. Then there was another picture of some veck I thought I knew, and it was this Minister of the Inferior or Interior. It seemed that he had been doing a bit of boasting, looking forward to a nice crime-free era in which there would be no more fear of cowardly attacks from young hooligans and perverts and burglars and all that cal. (3.1.5)

Thought: The Government is content to usurp the individual liberties of its constituents to achieve peace and stability for the State.

"I think you can help dislodge this overbearing Government. To turn a decent young man into a piece of clockwork should not, surely, be seen as any triumph for any government, save one that boasts of its repressiveness." (3.1.21)

Thought: At the very least, F. Alexander and co. believe the Government is overbearing because it does not respect the individual liberties of its people, in addition to other reasons.

"Recruiting brutal young roughs for the police. Proposing debilitating and will-sapping techniques of conditioning… Before we know where we are we shall have the full apparatus of totalitarianism." (3.5.8)

Thought: F. Alexander fears that the State is under rule by a totalitarian Government. Here, he also exposes one of the ways this Government seeks to repress its people: it hires hoodlums (like Alex's droog Dim and kids like Billyboy) as police to scare ordinary citizens off the streets. This is like institutionalizing gangs.

"Would they like their sons to become what you, poor victim, have become? Will not the Government itself now decide what is and what is not crime and pump out the life and guts and will of whoever sees fit to displease the Government?" (3.5.10

Thought: A totalitarian Government defers to no external system of right and wrong; it makes up its own criteria and imposes them upon its people.

"The tradition of liberty means all. The common people will let it go, oh yes. They will sell liberty for a quieter life. That is why they must be prodded, prodded— Eat well, poor boy, poor victim of the modern world." (3.5.12)

Thought: The Government opposes individual liberties and will sacrifice them for the collective good.

DEATH TO THE GOVERNMENT (3.5.42)

Thought: The people's hatred of the Government is one good sign of how repressive it is. Of course, this is usually not spoken out loud and is, in this case, written on a subversive pamphlet.

"It said they had done great wrong to you. It said how the Government drove you to try and do yourself in." (3.6.11)

Thought: It is clear that the Minister of the Interior's subsequent public apology is only for PR reasons, not made because he or the Government actually feels they have done anything wrong. This is yet another sign of a repressive, totalitarian government.

"He had this idea," said the Min. "He was a menace. We put him away for his own protection. And also," he said, "for yours." (3.6.69)

Thought: In actuality, the Government does not put F. Alexander away for being a "menace" or for his "own protection," but rather for being a political dissident, a "menace" to the Government's power. No totalitarian power would ever tolerate such an ideological opponent.

Transformation Quotes

"Common criminals like this unsavoury crowd"--(that meant me, brothers, as well as the others, who were real prestoopnicks and treacherous with it)--"can best be dealt with on a purely curative basis. Kill the criminal reflex, that's all. Full implementation in a year's time. Punishment means nothing to them, you can see that. They enjoy their so-called punishment. They start murdering each other." (2.2.17)

Thought: This "curative" approach seeks to transform "common criminals" like Alex altogether, rendering them incapable of committing crimes.

"All right, all right," said this big veck. Then he turned to the Governor and said: "You can use him as a trail-blazer. He's young, bold, vicious. Brodsky will deal with him tomorrow and you can sit in and watch Brodsky. It works all right, don't worry about that. This vicious young hoodlum will be transformed out of all recognition." And those hard slovos, brothers, were like the beginning of my freedom. (2.2.20-21)

Thought: Alex initially looks forward to undergoing the Reclamation Treatment, hoping to beat the system. Little does he know that he'll be transformed – no, eliminated – entirely.

"You felt ill this afternoon," he said, "because you're getting better. When we're healthy we respond to the presence of the hateful with fear and nausea. You're becoming healthy, that's all. You'll be healthier still this time tomorrow." (2.5.13)

Thought: It is noteworthy here that Dr. Brodsky treats Alex as a sick being, needing to be transformed so that he might act normally or "humanly" towards violence and crime.

"Today, old friend, we are letting you walk." (2.6.28)

Thought: Here's Alex's first step towards being transformed by Ludovico's Technique. The "old friend" also suggests that the doctors are welcoming Alex back into "their world."

"Aha. At this stage, gentlemen, we introduce the subject himself. He is, as you will perceive, fit and well nourished. He comes straight from a night's sleep and a good breakfast, undrugged, unhypnotized. Tomorrow we send him with confidence out into the world again, as decent a lad as you would meet on a May morning, inclined to the kindly word and the helpful act. What a change is here, gentlemen, from the wretched hoodlum the State committed to unprofitable punishment some two years ago, unchanged after two years. Unchanged, do I say? Not quite. Prison taught him the false smile, the rubbed hands of hypocrisy, the fawning greased obsequious leer. Other vices it taught him, as well as confirming him in those he had long practiced before. But gentlemen, enough of words. Actions speak louder than. Action now. Observe, all." (2.7.2)

Thought: Alex has been so thoroughly transformed that the doctors (as well as the Government) will send him into the world with full "confidence." Do you suppose that a treatment program with a "curative" or "transformational" objective is superior to one that is merely exists for deterrence or restitution purposes?

"He will be your true Christian," Dr. Brodsky was creeching out, "ready to turn the other cheek, ready to be crucified rather than crucify, sick to the very heart at the thought even of killing a fly." And that was right, brothers, because when he said that I thought of killing a fly and felt just that tiny bit sick, but I pushed the sickness and pain back by thinking of the fly being fed with bits of sugar and looked after like a bleeding pet and all that cal. "Reclamation," he creeched. "Joy before the Angels of God."
"The point is," this Minister of the Inferior was saying real gromky, "that it works." (2.7.24-25)

Thought: Alex has been transformed into a Christian, or at least a person who ostensibly performs Christian-like deeds. What is the difference?

What it said underneath my picture was that here was the first graduate from the new State Institute for Reclamation of Criminal Types, cured of his criminal instincts in a fortnight only, now a good law-fearing citizen and all that cal. Then I viddied there was a very boastful article about this Ludovico's Technique and how clever the Government was and all that cal. Then there was another picture of some veck I thought I knew, and it was this Minister of the Inferior or Interior. It seemed that he had been doing a bit of boasting, looking forward to a nice crime-free era in which there would be no more fear of cowardly attacks from young hooligans and perverts and burglars and all that cal. (3.1.5)

Thought: The Government views Alex as having been transformed and cured of his criminal instincts. The deeper message here is that the Government is content with usurping the individual liberties of its constituents to achieve peace and stability for the State.

"And what do I get out of this? Do I get cured of the way I am? Do I find myself able to slooshy the old Choral Symphony without being sick once more? Can I live like a normal jeezny again?" (3.5.13)

Thought: All Alex truly wants is to be transformed back to his former state, so that he may enjoy classical music again.

"Deep hypnopaedia... you seem to be cured." (3.6.48)

Thought: Yet again, Alex has been transformed. But this time, he has been transformed – or rather, restored – back to his old self.

But what was the matter with me these days was that I didn't like care much. It was like something soft getting into me and I could not pony why. What I wanted these days I did not know. (3.7.32)

Thought: This is the first sign of Alex's future personal transformation. This passage shows just how discontent he is with the status quo. He is looking for more.

That's what it's going to be then, brothers, as I come to the like end of this tale… I was young. But now as I end this story, brothers, I am not young, not no longer, oh no. Alex like growth up, oh yes. (2.7.57)

Thought: Not only has Alex finally answered the question that has appeared more than a dozen times throughout the book, but he has also definitively declared that he is young no longer. Wow.

Violence Quotes

My endeavour shall be, in such future as stretches out its snowy and lilywhite arms to me before the nozh overtakes or the blood spatters its final chorus in twisted metal and smashed glass on the highroad, to not get loveted again. Which is fair speeching. (1.4.21)

Thought: Notice that Alex's speech, when he talks of violence and gore and blood, is particularly flowery and aesthetic. It would seem obvious that he takes much aesthetic delight in violence.

…and that made the old veck start moaning a lot then, then out comes the blood, my brothers, real beautiful. So all we did then was to pull his outer platties off, stripping him down to his vest and long underpants (very starry; Dim smecked his head off near), and then Pete kicks him lovely in his pot. (1.1.22)

Thought: Again, Alex's descriptions of pain and blood have a particularly aesthetic quality. His light adjectives also show just how much he delights in violence.

And, my brothers, it was real satisfaction to me to waltz--left two three, right two three--and carve left cheeky and right cheeky, so that like two curtains of blood seemed to pour out at the same time, one on either side of his fat filthy oily snout in the winter starlight. Down this blood poured in like red curtains (1.2.8)

Thought: Why do you suppose Burgess seeks to emphasize the aesthetic qualities of violence so much in this book? This passage contains a solid hint.

We fillied round what was called the backtown for a bit, scaring old vecks and cheenas that were crossing the roads and zigzagging after cats and that. Then we took the road west. There wasn't much traffic about, so I kept pushing the old noga through the floorboards near, and the Durango 95 ate up the road like spaghetti. Soon it was winter trees and dark, my brothers, with a country dark, and at one place I ran over something big with a snarling toothy rot in the head-lamps, then it screamed and squelched under and old Dim at the back near laughed his gulliver off--"Ho ho ho"--at that. Then we saw one young malchick with his sharp, lubbilubbing under a tree, so we stopped and cheered at them, then we bashed into them both with a couple of half-hearted tolchocks, making them cry, and on we went. What we were after now was the old surprise visit. That was a real kick and good for smecks and lashings of the ultra-violent. (1.2.12)

Thought: Is Alex bored, delinquent, or just purely evil? What has caused him to take such delight in violence? This passage makes us wonder whether he sees it as an art form.

Next time it's going to be the barry place and all my work ruined. If you have no consideration for your horrible self you at least might have some for me, who have sweated over you. A big black mark, I tell you in confidence, for every one we don't reclaim, a confession of failure for every one of you that ends up in the stripy hole."
"I've been doing nothing I shouldn't, sir," I said. "The millicents have nothing on me, brother, sir I mean."
"Cut out this clever talk about millicents," said P.R. Deltoid very weary, but still rocking. "Just because the police have not picked you up lately doesn't, as you very well know, mean you've not been up to some nastiness. (1.4.14-16)

Thought: Alex sees a criminal as someone who gets caught doing something bad. This is to be juxtaposed with P.R. Deltoid's view that anyone who commits bad deeds is a criminal.

But, brothers, this biting of their toe-nails over what is the cause of badness is what turns me into a fine laughing malchick. They don't go into the cause of goodness, so why the other shop? If lewdies are good that's because they like it, and I wouldn't ever interfere with their pleasures, and so of the other shop. And I was patronizing the other shop. More, badness is of the self, the one, the you or me on our oddy knockies, and that self is made by old Bog or God and is his great pride and radosty. But the not-self cannot have the bad, meaning they of the government and the judges and the schools cannot allow the bad because they cannot allow the self. And is not our modern history, my brothers, the story of brave malenky selves fighting these big machines? I am serious with you, brothers, over this. But what I do I do because I like to do. (1.4.21)

Thought: Here, Alex is explaining how he commits violence for violence's sake! (It's tough to read this without feeling pretty disturbed.)

I felt the old tigers leap in me and then I leapt on these two young ptitsas. This time they thought nothing fun and stopped creeching with high mirth, and had to submit to the strange and weird desires of Alexander the Large which, what with the Ninth and the hypo jab, were choodessny and zammechat and very demanding, O my brothers. But they were both very very drunken and could hardly feel very much.

When the last movement had gone round for the second time with all the banging and creeching about Joy Joy Joy Joy, then these two young ptitsas were not acting the big lady sophisto no more. They were like waking up to what was being done to their malenky persons and saying that they wanted to go home and like I was a wild beast. They looked like they had been in some big bitva, as indeed they had, and were all bruised and pouty. (1.4.34-35)

Thought: It appears that Alex's enjoyment of violence is heightened by great "violent" music. He comes close to almost having a religious experience here with the rape of the 10-year-olds, all while Beethoven's 9th Symphony is playing. That, in and of itself, is very disturbing. Why is music so significant to Alex?

I would read of these starry yahoodies tolchocking each other and then peeting their Hebrew vino and getting on to the bed with their wives' like hand-maidens, real horrorshow. That kept me going, brothers. I didn't so much kopat the later part of the book, which is more like all preachy govoreeting than fighting and the old in-out. (2.1.9)

Thought: Alex delights in the sex and violence depicted in the Old Testament. Sex and violence is ubiquitous there!

So they all stood around while I cracked at this prestoopnick in the near dark. I fisted him all over, dancing about with my boots on though unlaced, and then I tripped him and he went crash crash on to the floor. I gave him one real horrorshow kick on the gulliver and he went ohhhh, then he sort of snorted off to like sleep… (2.2.10)

Thought: There is something counter-intuitive about beating a guy up in jail and later killing him. Perhaps this is just what criminals do, but something tells us that only hardened, unreformable, and unrepentant criminals (like the ones the Governor and the Minister of the Interior speak about) do this.

He just sort of looked right through us poor plennies, saying, in a very beautiful real educated goloss: "The Government cannot be concerned any longer with outmoded penological theories. Cram criminals together and see what happens. You get concentrated criminality, crime in the midst of punishment. Soon we may be needing all our prison space for political offenders." (2.2.17)

Thought: Forget the criminals, we need the space for political dissidents! These are the true colors of the Government. Aside from not caring about individual criminals, the Government seeks to free up space for the forces of subversion it seems to have imprisoned. What better way to quell discontent than to jail all the dissidents?

"Common criminals like this unsavoury crowd"--(that meant me, brothers, as well as the others, who were real prestoopnicks and treacherous with it)--"can best be dealt with on a purely curative basis. Kill the criminal reflex, that's all. Full implementation in a year's time. Punishment means nothing to them, you can see that. They enjoy their so-called punishment. They start murdering each other." (2.2.17)

Thought: The Government says that hardened criminals don't care about being jailed or punished. Hardened criminals need to be "cured" of their criminal instinct. In case you can't tell, this is Government propaganda to further its own agenda of freeing space in the prisons for all the political dissidents.

Language and Communication Quotes

"These grahzny sodding veshches that come out of my gulliver and my plott," I said, "that's what it is."
"Quaint," said Dr. Brodsky, like smiling, "the dialect of the tribe. Do you know anything of its provenance, Branom?"
"Odd bits of old rhyming slang," said Dr. Branom, who did not look quite so much like a friend any more. "A bit of gipsy talk, too. But most of the roots are Slav. Propaganda. Subliminal penetration." (2.6.13-15)

Thought: AHA! So these are the roots of nadsat, as it were. Can you think of any significance that might be attached to it's being a predominantly Slavic-influenced language? Is Burgess referring to his own process, as an author, with the "subliminal penetration" idea? What role does nadsat play as a literary device in this book?

...so I said in a very refined manner of speech, a real gentleman's goloss:
"Pardon, madam, most sorry to disturb you, but my friend and me were out for a walk, and my friend has taken bad all of a sudden with a very troublesome turn, and he is out there on the road dead out and groaning. Would you have the goodness to let me use your telephone to telephone for an ambulance?"
The devotchka sort of hesitated and then said: "Wait." Then she went off, and my three droogs had got out of the auto quiet and crept up horrorshow stealthy, putting their maskies on now, then I put mine on, then it was only a matter of me putting in the old rooker and undoing the chain, me having softened up this devotchka with my gent's goloss, so that she hadn't shut the door like she should have done, us being strangers of the night. (1.2.13-15)

Thought: Alex uses his voice and speech to his advantage in deceiving others. The change in the manner in which he speaks essentially makes him a chameleon.

"Strange, strange, that manner of voice pricks me. We've come into contact before, I'm sure we have." (3.5.21)

Thought: Ahh…the subtle workings of language and speech!

"Life is a very wonderful thing," said Dr. Branom in a like very holy goloss. "The processes of life, the make-up of the human organism, who can fully understand these miracles…" (2.5.9)

Thought: Alex describes Dr. Branom as speaking in a very "holy" tone. What does this mean, exactly? How does this shed light on the content of the speech to come?

He just sort of looked right through us poor plennies, saying, in a very beautiful real educated goloss: "The Government cannot be concerned any longer with outmoded penological theories. Cram criminals together and see what happens. You get concentrated criminality, crime in the midst of punishment. Soon we may be needing all our prison space for political offenders." (2.2.17)

Thought: Can tone and language lend authority to the speaker? Do you think it is important to speak well? How has Alex learned to speak so well as to fool others?

Plot Analysis

Classic Plot Analysis

Initial Situation
Alex and his entourage tear up the city and countryside, taking sheer joy engaging in ultra-violent crimes like mugging, robbery, gang fights, grand theft auto, vandalism, rape, and murder. He and his criminal friends represent the violent "modern youth" that threaten the stability of the State.
Alex and his entourage's crimes set the scene for the book. The raping and pillaging show just how heartlessly brutal and evil these teens are. We also get tuned in to just what a problem these "modern youth" like Alex and the gang can be to the State.

Conflict
Dim and Georgie, unhappy with Alex's assertion of arrogant authority over the group, challenge his leadership. The three get in a fight.
As a naturally aggressive alpha-male, Alex likes to assert his authority and leadership over his

friends. But when Alex punches Dim for being "annoying," Dim and Georgie speak out against Alex's authority. A fight ensues and, voila, we have "conflict."

Complication

Alex runs into trouble trying to assert his manhood in the Manse "job." The police arrive just as Alex is temporarily blinded by Dim, who's giving payback to Alex for beating him up earlier in the night.

It gets complicated. Alex, rendered a bit insecure by Dim and Georgie's opposition to this authority, wants to show off a little bit, by playing "Big Man on Campus" at the cat-lady's mansion. Little does he know, though, that cats are his bad luck charm. The cat-lady – before she gets beaten to death by Alex, of course – calls the police. And just as Alex is scrambling to get out of the mansion, he meets Dim, chain in hand. What goes around comes around, and Dim whacks Alex in the eye with his chain – payback style. Alex is temporarily blinded and therefore immobile, making him an easy capture for the police.

Climax

Alex is thrown into jail for fourteen years. Two years into his sentence, Alex kills another prisoner and is chosen to be the first subject to undergo the Reclamation Treatment employing the Ludovico's Technique – still in its experimental stage.

Never would we have thought that this droog would be thrown into jail. He definitely deserved it, though. And he definitely needs it. Of course, the killing of his cellmate, while uncalled for, doesn't really surprise us. As Alex himself notes, his new cellmate marked a kind of new beginning and hope for him – and that suggests "climax" to us.

Suspense

Alex gets discharged from prison a half-person, now unable to commit a crime. His past quickly catches up with him as he suffers beatings at the hands of past victims and ex-friends.

What's it going to be then, eh? In other words, what will Alex do now that he's out of jail? Unable to even think of violence, how will he defend himself against the rest of the criminals on the street? These questions make this stage totally suspenseful.

Denouement

Alex gets caught up in F. Alexander's political agenda, which aims at overthrowing the current Government. Alex almost dies in a rather complicated way.

With all the violence over with in this book, we're now onto "falling action." Alex is left to die in the snow; he stumbles upon a cottage in the country; the inhabitant of the cottage is a political dissident; he wants to incorporate Alex into his plans against the Government.

Conclusion

Restored to his old self again, Alex runs into an old friend, Pete, who is now happily married and enjoying his life. Inspired by Pete's apparent satisfaction with his life, Alex also aspires to lead a "normal" life, and looks forward to a wife and a son.

Seemingly immediate, this transformation Alex goes through is not necessarily instantaneous. A nice transition from violent, unthinking youth to calm, thoughtful adult (he turned 18 not so long ago), Alex provides us with a nice conclusion to an otherwise unsettling story.

Booker's Seven Basic Plots Analysis: Overcoming the Monster

Anticipation Stage and "Call"

The "monster" is the threat of becoming a "clockwork orange" – an extremely visceral threat that Alex faces as a result of having undergone Ludovico's Technique. After all, a man who is unable to exercise freedom of choice ceases to be a man – and Alex is trying to rebel against the monstrosity of it.

Interestingly enough, this Basic Plot of Booker's does not apply until Part Two of the book, meaning that part one mostly provides background and buildup for the ordeal to come. Nonetheless, the "monster" has been anticipated in part one; for instance, when Alex reads from F. Alexander's loose manuscript entitled *A Clockwork Orange*. Most of part two has Alex set up to embody the highly feared "monster." In any case, it is definitely something that everyone (except the State, we suppose) fights against, and so is an appropriate "monster."

Dream Stage

Serendipitously, Alex hooks up with F. Alexander, whose plans of overthrowing the Government are already underway.

Picture this. You've become your worst fear – say, a werewolf. You get beat up and left out to die. You stumble towards a random cottage, and a scientist inside is brewing a solution which promises to transform werewolves back into humans. You pinch yourself and wonder, wait, is this a dream? Anyway, that's how Alex finds F. Alexander.

Frustration Stage

Unfortunately, F. Alexander recognizes Alex as the rapist and murderer of his wife, arousing within him a thirst for vengeance against Alex, in addition to a desire to use Alex as a pawn against the Government.

Of course, just when things are going well, complications are bound to arise. In this stage, just as Alex prepares to sign the confession/article F. Alexander has drafted for him as part of their shared subversive plans, F. Alexander realizes that he has unfinished business (personal, of course) with Alex. Thus, instead of executing the original plan (i.e., publish something that makes the Government look irredeemably evil), he comes up with a new plan.

Nightmare Stage

Cornered by the classical music blasting through the wall of his locked quarters, Alex leaps from the multi-storied building, perhaps to his death.

The new plan by F. Alexander and his associates is the nightmare that Alex must confront. Unable to endure the pain of classical music as acquired through his associative learning treatment, Alex has no choice but to leap from a tall building to escape. This is not unlike Winston Smith's confrontation with rats (his #1 fear) in George Orwell's *1984*. Can you imagine that: facing your worst nightmare and having to choose between it and…death?

Thrilling Escape from Death and Death of the Monster

Luckily, Alex does not die, and the circumstances lead to the State's reversal of Ludovico's Technique on Alex, restoring him back to his old self.

Fortunately, Alex does not die from the jump and instead enjoys a few weeks of being an invalid

in bed. His nightmarish journey gains public attention, and the State's doctors work to restore him in an effort to please the public and gain votes for the upcoming election. A clockwork orange no more, Alex is turned back into the evil urchin that delights in violence. The icing on the cake is that F. Alexander has been put away for being a lunatic out for blood.

Three Act Plot Analysis

Act I
Alex wages violent crimes in both the city and the countryside of a futuristic English state.

Act II
Alex is imprisoned for his crimes, and forced to undergo behavioral therapy to be "cured" of his evil tendencies once and for all.

Act III
After many complications, Alex finds himself interested in leading a peaceful and "normal" life, even after the capacity for evil has been restored in him.

Study Questions

1. Why is freedom of choice such an important concept in this book? Do you believe "choice" is a predominantly American ideal? What would people in Communist China (or anywhere else with much stricter censorship) think about the matter? What would they think about the book?
2. Would the violent, nadsat-speaking modern youth be better off with RPGs (role-playing games) or worse off? In what ways could RPGs influence their behavior positively or negatively?
3. What does moral choice have to do with the concept of good and evil? How would you define good and of evil? Good and bad? Can a person who doesn't really know how to commit crime be viewed as a good person, or must she affirmatively decline to commit crimes to be viewed as such?
4. Are brainwashed people no longer people? Are they more like robots or children? What about people who have been indoctrinated with a certain religious philosophy; can they still be considered autonomous? How about people who have been manipulated subliminally through decades upon decades of masterful advertising?
5. Can language shape thought? Does society (and what happens in it) shape language and communication? If the youth in the book were not communicating in nadsat – which, arguably, may be conducive to violence – is it possible that they might act less violently? What is the importance of nadsat to the tenets of the book?
6. Based on what Alex thinks about in the last chapter, do you suppose that children can also be considered clockwork oranges? What is the significance of that reference? Why does Burgess reference it throughout the book? Who is the best example of a clockwork orange,

and why?

7. Do you see a connection between violence and music? Why or why not? Why do you suppose Alex links the two? How coincidental is it that Ludovico's Technique also involves music? What is the significance of that?

Characters

All Characters

Alex Character Analysis

The protagonist-narrator of his violent and almost sci-fi adventure, Alex starts out as a fifteen-year-old gang leader of "modern youth" hell-bent on raping and pillaging. By the end of the book, he experiences a moral and personal transformation that seems completely out of place with his character. Well, not so much out of place if you are paying attention to his struggles and revelations.

A true dichotomy in every sense of the word, Alex is at once innocently endearing and purely evil, immature in his actions yet worldly in his thoughts about government, a connoisseur of classical music and an inflictor of lowly brutality. He dresses in the "heighth of fashion," hangs out in the most popular bars, and speaks in nadsat – a stylized dialectic to which only the coolest "modern youth" are privy. In other words, he's a handful of both trouble and intrigue.

Alex believes that evil is the natural state for all human beings. In choosing to be evil, he is choosing to be human. The totalitarian State disagrees with him, however, as it tries to deprive him of his choice to act violently at all. Thus, Alex's struggles against the State represent the struggles of human nature against automaton, freedom against determinism, individualism against mass repression, Etc. In the final chapter, as Alex re-becomes who he was and resolves to be different, he emerges triumphant against all that Burgess finds wrong with the world, morally speaking.

Alex Timeline and Summary

- The book opens with our narrator and protagonist, Alex, along with his "droogs" (that would be "friends"), Pete, Georgie, and Dim, sitting in the Korova Milkbar contemplating what trouble to get in to on this particularly dark and chilly winter evening.
- Alex and his entourage are drinking "milk-plus," meaning milk laced with some type of hallucinogen or other drug. Alex describes the milk-plus experience as one that either gives you a nice fireworks-in-the-sky kind of buzz, or else a lot of courage and strength.

- Alex describes his entourage as dressed in the "heighth of fashion," which, at the time, meant a pair of black tights, a big belt, a cropped jacket without lapels but with big, built-up shoulders, a hat, and great boots for kicking.
- Alex observes three girls at the bar, also dressed in the heighth of fashion.
- The man sitting next to Alex is quite drunk and is talking gibberish about Aristotle. Alex isn't amused at all, but finds it rather cowardly that this grown dude next to him could get so wasted.
- The milk-plus starts to kick in for our boys.
- "Out out out out!" Alex shouts, and the entourage leaves the bar for Marghanita Boulevard.
- They turn down Boothby Avenue, looking for trouble.
- Alex approaches the first victim of the night, first calling him "brother." The man has some books with him, and, flipping through them, Alex insinuates that they are books of pornography, and teases the man about it.
- As the man tries to grab his books back, Alex and co. beat him up, strip off his clothes, and go through his trousers for money.
- The boys are off to the Duke of New York bar on Amis Avenue to spend what money they've taken from the old man.
- They come upon three or four old ladies at the bar – real drunk – and buy them drinks and snacks in exchange for an alibi.
- The boys, led by Alex, leave the bar to a cigs and sweets shop on the corner of Attlee Avenue.
- They put on their high-quality, life-like masks.
- Barging inside the store, Alex beats up Mother Slouse, the wife of the shopkeeper, kicking her, ripping her clothes, staring at her naked breasts, and contemplating sex – until he resolves that this is for later on in the evening.
- The boys clean the register, grab a few packs of the very best cigarettes (they call them "cancers") and jet back into the Duke of New York in less than ten minutes altogether.
- The boys buy the alibi ladies more drinks.
- Half an hour goes by before the police come to question the patrons of the bar for potential information.
- The boys sneer at the police, while the ladies provide them with their purchased alibi.
- Outside of the Duke of New York, the boys encounter a singing drunk.
- And, of course, he too gets a bloody beating from Alex and co.
- Alex's posse moves on, coming upon Billyboy and his five droogs right around the Municipal Power Plant.
- Alex hates how Billyboy always smells like stale oil, and challenges him and entourage to a fight.
- Alex puts his cut-throat knife to work, using it to slit down the front of one of the opponent's jackets until he's bare-bellied...
- Alex and co. are of course coming out on top in the fight, until they hear sirens.
- All the boys scatter. Alex and his friends run to a dark alley to catch their breath.
- With the sirens gone, Alex leads his friends to Priestley Place, and then to the Filmdrome (theatre) parking lot to look for a getaway car.
- They steal a new-ish Durango 95 easily.
- The boys drive recklessly, running over animals large and small, and terrorizing the townspeople.
- The moon is bright and shiny as Alex decides that it's time for the "old surprise visit."

Driving into the countryside, he stops the car just before entering "a sort of a village," in front of a small cottage that has "HOME" on a plate hanging on the gate.

- Alex knocks on the door of the cottage and a woman answers.
- Speaking like a gentleman, Alex asks to use the phone to call an ambulance for his friend, who has supposedly fallen ill just outside the cottage.
- Alex asks for a glass of water to soothe his friend.
- Alex and co. put on their masks and barge in while the woman goes to fetch the water.
- Inside the cottage, Alex picks up a pile of typewriter paper and starts to mock the writer.
- Alex tears up the manuscript.
- Alex orders Georgie and Pete to drop the food and grab the writer so he can watch what they're about to do.
- Dim holds the writer's wife down, while Alex begins to rip off her clothes.
- Excited, Alex gets undressed and starts to "plunge."
- Alex finishes, and Dim takes his turn with the woman while Alex holds her down.
- Alex howls, "Out out out out!"
- The tired Alex lets Georgie take the wheel of the waiting car. The gang heads back to town, running over the odd animal here and there.
- Running out of fuel, the boys abandon the Durango, pushing it into the wasteland waters. They catch the train.
- The boys get off at Center station, and walk back to Korova Milkbar.
- Tired, they realize they should get home soon, since they are still growing boys and have school the next day.
- Opera music is playing, and Alex, being very sensitive to classical music, shivers upon hearing it.
- Dim interrupts Alex's moment with a bit of vulgarity, causing Alex to cuss him out.
- Not enough, apparently, Alex leans over Georgie to punch Dim in the mouth.
- Alex chastises him for being a "bastard with no manners."
- Dim says he doesn't want to be Alex's brother and friend anymore.
- Asserting his authority, Alex challenges Dim to a fight outside.
- Alex retorts that Dim has to learn his place, since Alex is the leader.
- An impassioned Alex re-asserts his leadership and authority, stating that even among friends, somebody has to be in charge.
- Alone now, Alex walks back to his parents' flat at 18A, Municipal Flatblock, between Kingsley Avenue and Wilsonsway.
- He takes the stairs, finally arriving on the 18th floor to a dark and quiet apartment.
- Alex gulps up the milk and dinner that have been laid out for him.
- After brushing his teeth, he enters his bedroom.
- He looks proudly at the flags and manners on the walls, his many music discs and stereo. He puts on some classical music, which gives him instantaneous bliss. He finally drifts off to dreamland to some J.S. Bach, with thoughts about a clockwork orange.
- Alex comes to at 8am and feels pretty bad physically.
- Alex has a headache and wants to sleep it off instead.
- Alex drifts back to dreamland and has a nightmare.
- The doorbell rings.
- It's P. R. Deltoid, Alex's Post-Corrective Adviser, stopping by to check up on him.
- Alex explains that he has ditched school because of a rather intolerable pain in the head, and offers P. R. Deltoid some tea.

- Alex denies that he's done anything worthy of worry. Yeah, right.
- Confronted by P. R. Deltoid, Alex continues with the "I don't know what you're talking about" approach.
- After P. R. Deltoid leaves, Alex dismisses his warnings as silly. He now muses over the concepts of goodness and badness, wondering out loud that modern youths like himself commit crimes for the sheer fun of it. Alex then waxes philosophy and concludes that if his government does not allow bad behavior, then it denies its constituents a life to live and ceases to be a government at all, by definition.
- Alex has his breakfast and reads the paper.
- Alex gets dressed with the radio on. A familiar string quartet plays and Alex is overjoyed.
- On his way out to the record store to pick up a copy of Beethoven's Symphony No. 9, Alex notes that the day is very different from the night.
- Alex gets to Melodia, the record store, at Taylor Place, and eyes the two ten-year-old girls in there, also playing hooky.
- He asks the storekeeper, old Andy, for Beethoven's Ninth.
- While paying for his new record, one of the pop music girls flirts with Alex. Alex gets an idea in his head, and promptly flirts back, promising food and music if they would leave with him.
- Alex buys the girls, named Marty and Sonietta, spaghetti, sausages, cream-puffs, banana-splits, and hot chocolate. Then he orders a taxi to bring them back to Municipal Flatblock 18A.
- At his parents' flat, Alex gives the girls a lot of Scotch and plays for them the pop music they have brought. He encourages them to drink more and quickly.
- Alex puts on Beethoven's Ninth, and he leaps on the girls, raping them to the sweet sounds of Ode to Joy.
- Alex lets them gather their things and kicks them out of the flat. He promptly dozes off to more Ode to Joy.
- It is almost 7:30pm when Alex comes to.
- Putting on his coat, he peers out, bidding his parents hello, as their only loving son.
- Alex takes a shower, then joins his parents at the dinner table.
- His father asks about his night job; Alex responds that it's just odd things, here and there.
- Alex assures him that he's not up to no good. He reaches in his pockets and puts some money on the table, offering it to his parents and telling them to buy some Scotch at a bar with it.
- By the time Alex gets to the bottom of the stairs Municipal Flatblock, his droogs are already waiting…yes, dressed in the heighth of fashion.
- The entourage lets Alex know that it got worried when he was late.
- Alex recounts his day, both the headache and the visit from P. R. Deltoid, but conveniently leaves out the girls.
- Georgie gets sarcastic with Alex, or so Alex charges.
- Alex goes on a rant about leadership and sarcasm, and insults Dim meanwhile.
- Georgie defends Dim, asking Alex not to pick on him again, staying that there is a "new way" that the posse has agreed to.
- Alex gets flippant. New way? No way.
- Seeing that he is outnumbered, Alex smiles and plays along, asking Georgie about his plan.
- Alex hears Beethoven's Violin Concerto on the radio of a passing car, and felt a violent

surge in his veins. He draws his knife on Georgie.
- Georgie draws his knife, and the two have at it until Alex cuts Georgie's hand.
- Now Dim uncoils his chain and lunges at Alex. Alex gets hit on the back, but manages to get back up and slash Dim's left wrist.
- Alex challenges a worried Pete. Pete is afraid that Dim's going to bleed to death.
- The emerging leader, Alex, now binds Dim's wrist with some cloth in his pocket. Declaring himself master and leader again, Alex gets his friends to the Duke of New York for a calm time.
- They see the alibi ladies, who are ultra-friendly with them.
- Alex confirms with Georgie that all is forgotten.
- Georgie suggests that his "mansize" plan for the night is to rob the Mansion (or the Manse) where a very old woman lives with her cats and valuables.
- Alex agrees that it's a great idea.
- Alex promises the alibi girls more drinks when they get back in ten minutes.
- Foreshadowing: Alex says he "led [his] three droogs out to [his] doom."
- Alex and co. arrive at the Manse, or the site for the night's job.
- Alex, anxious to prove himself as a worthwhile leader, runs with the plan.
- Alex pleads with her to help his ill-fated friend.
- Alex pretends to retreat, all the while narrating how the woman's suspicions are well-founded, since the streets are a dangerous place.
- In the dark, the gang reconvenes. Alex, still anxious to show them who's who, suggests that he stand on Dim's shoulders to open a window for all of them.
- The plan works! Alex cracks the glass and hops into a room full of beds, cupboards, boxes, and books.
- Once inside, Alex decides that he'll do the job (which includes robbing, raping, and possibly killing) alone, to impress his droogs…so they can really learn all about leadership when he opens the front door bearing all the valuables.
- Eyeing the stairs going down to the hall, Alex waltzes down there and startles the cat-lady.
- Alex gets distracted by a stone bust of Beethoven.
- Not seeing the milk saucers on the floor, he trips.
- WHACK! Cat-lady cracks his head with her stick.
- Alex grabs her stick and pulls her down on the floor, still holding onto the table-cloth.
- More struggling ensues. Tripping on another milk saucer, Alex is down, being scratched by the cats and whacked on the head by their owner's walking stick.
- Fed up, Alex takes a silver statue and bashes the cat-lady across the head with it.
- Police sirens sound in the distance. Alex runs for the front door.
- He is met with Dim and Dim's chain.
- Dim whips Alex in the head with his chain, blinding him momentarily, and then runs off.
- Alex stumbles in the hallway, groping at things blindly, until the policemen come upon him.
- He realizes that Dim and co. have sold him out.
- Alex yells at the police that his friends – his former brothers – forced him to do this.
- Alex is taken away in the squad car.
- He insists that his friends put him up to the test with this last job.
- Alex is dragged into a brightly lit office with whitewashed walls.
- Alex demands a lawyer, but gets laughed at and punched instead.
- Alex almost throws up, but holds it back.
- He retaliates with a kick and punch.

- After that, the four policemen gang up on him and beat him until he cries apologies.
- P. R. Deltoid comes to visit Alex.
- Alex tries to explain that he was influenced by his no-good friends.
- P. R. Deltoid spits in Alex's face, then wipes his wet lips with the back of his hand. Alex thanks P. R. Deltoid, who leaves promptly.
- The police now push Alex to make a statement that would then be turned into a signed confession. So, Alex gushes on about the ultra-violence and the rape for pages on end, making sure to include his so-called friends.
- Alex is then kicked, punched, and bullied off to a holding cell with ten or twelve other criminals, most of them drunk. Two of these criminals are "queer" and immediately try to molest him. Alex manages to fight them off with the help of a cop.
- Exhausted, Alex drifts off thinking about Beethoven's Ninth.
- A cop comes to wake Alex up from the other end of the holding cell. Reluctantly, Alex goes to him.
- But before the cop can open his mouth, Alex knows the scoop: the cat-lady has died in the hospital; apparently, Alex cracked her a bit too hard.
- Alex thinks about all the cats, now orphaned, having no mistress who will feed them.
- Alex realizes that he has committed murder, and reveals that he has done so at the ripe old age of fifteen.
- Alex narrates from cell number 84F in Staja.
- Alex has been sentenced to fourteen years.
- Alex reflects upon the two hard years in the human zoo. On a daily basis, he has dealt with wardens that kick and beat him, perverts who wish to rape him, all the while toiling away in the factory making matchboxes and doing exercises in the courtyard. Sometimes, he has to suffer through guest speeches on beetles or the Milky Way for "education" purposes, but during these speeches, he keeps himself entertained thinking about happier, ultra-violent days.
- One day, Alex is informed that his friend Georgie died while involved in some ultra-violence with Dim and Pete. The news pleases him.
- More time passes, and Alex adjusts to prison life. He has a new job playing the stereo for the prison chaplain during Sunday worship. He likes his new job.
- Alex reveals that the chaplain likes him because of his interest in the Bible. Alex especially delights in all the sex and violence he gets to read about in the Old Testament.
- Alex is not so partial to the New Testament because it gets a bit preachy for his taste.
- Alex excels at his new job, always ready with the record or the disc on queue.
- Alex takes the chance to ask the chaplain about a certain new "treatment" that gets one out of prison in no time at all, ensuring that one stays out of prison as well.
- Ludovico's Technique, answers the chaplain thoughtfully. He hesitantly cautions Alex that the program is just in its infancy.
- Alex answers that it must be starting to get used, because he sees the new white buildings they've been putting up adjacent to the Staja.
- Alex goes back to his cell after lunch to find that he has a new cellmate.
- Alex muses that his new cellmate marks the beginning of his getting out of jail.
- That night, Alex wakes up to find the guy lying next to him in his bed, snoring and masturbating. Alex punches him as a part of a reflex.
- Alex punches the guy and the rest of his cellmates join in. Alex ends the fight by kicking the new prisoner in the head.

- Alex goes to bed, dreaming about Beethoven and Handel until the prison buzzer wakes him up.
- Alex touches the stiff body of the guy he kicked, now dead.
- The prisoners panic a bit, but decide that Alex is the main person responsible for his death.
- Alex retorts that everyone joined in on teaching the guy a lesson, so why should he take the fall?
- At 11am, the Governor and the Chief and other important-looking officials come for Alex. They chat among one another about whether the Government should move away from outmoded theories of dealing with criminals and embrace the a theory based on a "curative" view.
- Alex tries to butt in, but is shut down quickly.
- One of the official-looking people turns to the Governor and suggests that he take Alex to Brodsky, because Alex is young, bold, and vicious…and ought to be transformed out of recognition.
- To Alex, those words taste like freedom.
- That evening, the guards drag Alex down to the Governor's office.
- The Governor tells Alex that he is to be "transformed" starting tomorrow by enrolling in a two-week program which will end in his release.
- Alex expresses his gratitude.
- Alex signs a waiver granting the State the power to "reclaim" him.
- The next morning, Alex is brought to the new white building adjacent to Staja.
- Alex feels lucky upon seeing his own room.
- Alex asks what he'll be doing.
- Dr. Branom decides that Alex seems a bit under-nourished, probably due to the poor prison food.
- He suggests that Alex expect a shot after every meal.
- Alex lies in bed daydreaming about freedom, getting out, and getting a new gang together.
- He has a meal of hot roast-beef with mashed potatoes, followed by ice cream and tea for dessert. There's even a cigarette.
- This is the life, thinks Alex.
- Half an hour after his meal, a woman nurse with nice breasts comes in and gives him a shot in the arm.
- Some white coat now comes in with a wheelchair for Alex, who questions why it's necessary.
- He realizes soon thereafter that he's been feeling a bit weak.
- Alex enters a mind-blowing room with a giant silver screen, a dentist-looking chair, and lots of white coats. Still feeling weak, Alex has to crawl from the wheelchair into the dentist's chair.
- A white coat straps his head, hands, and feet down; the staff also attaches clips to his forehead so that his eyelids are forced to be open.
- Alex wonders out loud how "horrorshow" this film must be.
- Alex is forced to watch a film. He begins to feel ill in the stomach.
- A second film, and Alex is feeling pains all over his body and also wanting to throw up one minute and not the next. He begins to feel distress.
- They show him a third film. Alex reasons with himself that this film cannot be real, but he still feels just as sick.
- A fourth film shows an old woman shopkeeper being robbed by a lot of modern youth. The

- woman is being burned alive, and her shrieks make Alex want to vomit.
- The fifth film Alex views takes place during World War II. Alex feels now feels such horrible pain in his head and belly that he screams for the film to be stopped.
- Alex now refuses to describe the other films he's been forced to watch that afternoon, but he does let on that he believes Dr. Brodsky and Dr. Branom and all the white coats are sicker than any of the prisoners he's met.
- Finally, Alex is released – sick and tired and nauseous – back to his room.
- Alex realizes that the white coats must be doing something to make him ill, and wonders if it's the wires that are attached to him.
- A Discharge Officer comes in to question Alex's plans upon his release.
- Before exiting the room, the Discharge Officer challenges Alex to punch him in the face.
- Alex is puzzled, but attempts to punch the officer in the face anyhow.
- He immediately feels ill, thinking the whole thing pretty funny.
- After dinner, Alex goes to sleep and has a nightmare about one of the films he saw that afternoon.
- At the height of all the ultra-violence in the dream, he feels paralyzed and nauseated.
- Alex wakes up and attempts to get out of the room, only to find it locked and the windows barred. He realizes for the first time that there's no escaping from all of this.
- Worse, he does not dare to go back to sleep, not wanting to get sick.
- Soon enough, he is able to fall asleep anyhow, and thank goodness, he doesn't have to dream.
- This chapter opens with Alex screaming for the white coats to stop the film.
- Alex throws up while pleading with the white coats to stop the film and its musical accompaniment. He calls it a filthy unforgivable sin to play Beethoven's Symphony No. 5 while showing a Nazi film.
- Alex retreats, stating that he doesn't care about the ultra-violent films, but he won't forgive the white coats for playing Beethoven and Handel with the films.
- Alex squirms, saying that he's learned his lesson, and that his paradigm has been transformed. He's against violence, finally.
- Alex reasons that it must be the shot that's making him sick.
- The next day, Alex hits the nurse in order to avoid his shot.
- Alex then skips the minutiae in his descriptions of the film-viewing. He states that the days seem to blend together as he's shown the same likeness of ultra-violent films: Japanese torturers or Nazi shooters…whatever.
- Then, one morning Alex wakes up to have his breakfast and shot, and the nurse with the syringe does not come.
- Today, Alex was going to walk to the screening room accompanied by a white coat.
- No syringes? None needed.
- The film rolls, and Alex feels sick. But this time, he realizes that he can no longer blame the syringes for feeling sick and thirsty and full of aches. He realizes that the Ludovico stuff is like a vaccination, and that his blood has been poisoned against the ultra-violence.
- Alex cries and cries and cries…
- That night, he lies in bed alone, contemplating escape.
- He fakes illness, crying out to the doctors that he is dying…
- A jangle of keys at the door; Alex prepares to throw his fists at the first fool that opens the locked door.
- The problem is, Alex envisions his unsuspecting victim in pain. And a sickness arises in

- him as if it might kill him.
- Alex stumbles toward the bed in fear, moaning "urgh urgh urgh."
- Finally, while Alex lies there immobile, the white coat punches him in the face for his deceit.
- Alex learns that he has become a total wimp, and that now it feels better to him to be hit than to throw a punch.
- The fortnight is up for Alex. There's one real big day left. It's to be a "passing-out day."
- This morning, Alex's been given the clothes he was wearing on the night he was arrested, except now all nicely pressed. He's even been given his knife back.
- Led quietly to the same old room, Alex notices that the curtains have been drawn in front of the silver screen, and that the frosted viewing glass under the projection area has disappeared.
- The Staja Governor, the chaplain, the Minister of the Interior, the doctors, and the other white coats are all there.
- The lights go out. Two spotlights begin to shine.
- One shines on Alex; the other shines on a big dude he's never seen before.
- The man starts to insult Alex. Then he pinches Alex's nose, twists his ear…the pain stings!
- The dude challenges Alex to hit back.
- Alex reaches for his knife, but is immediately overwhelmed by images of blood gushing out of the guy. He realizes that he has to change his own perception of this adversary before he starts to get sick.
- Alex pleads with the man to take his cigarette, then his knife, then offers to clean his boots.
- Alex licks the dude's shoes. The audience roars with laughter.
- Alex screeches, what about me? Am I just an animal? Am I just a clockwork orange?
- Alex notes that the second actor, a woman, has nice breasts.
- Alex is aroused, and immediately thinks about raping her like a fierce savage.
- But a shot of sickness pierces through his daydream and he knows he has to think about something else before it takes over completely.
- Alex breaks into what seems like a Shakespearean sonnet, offering to worship and protect the young actress.
- Standing outside of the white building the next day, Alex recounts his last day inside it.
- On an empty stomach, Alex decides to grab some grub.
- Alex reads the morning paper. Alex throws the paper on the floor in a fit of rage.
- A homebound Alex looks forward to surprising his parents, all the while dreaming about the classical music he'll be able to listen to in bed.
- Alex opens the door to his home with the key he has in his pants; he finds himself confronted by three pairs of frightened eyes, belonging to his parents and to a stranger Alex has never seen before.
- Alex's parents started questioning him how he broke out of jail.
- Alex starts to explain, and the stranger starts to huff and puff…
- Alex questions the stranger: how long has he been there, what he does, etc. He looks to be thirty or forty, very ugly, very middle-class.
- Alex's dad interrupts to defend the stranger, Joe. He lives there now; he's renting Alex's room.
- Upon noticing that his stereo and discs are gone from his room, Alex screams out in pain, calling Joe a horrible bastard.
- A baffled Alex sits down.

- Alex retorts to Joe with profanity, and instantly feels pretty sick.
- Alex starts to cry, feeling very sorry for himself.
- In tears, Alex speaks out about how everyone just wants him to suffer.
- Alex staggers out the door, saying that he'll never be seen again. And that he wishes he were back in prison.
- Alex wanders into the disc shop he used to frequent.
- Alex wants to listen to a bit of the Mozart Number Forty in the listening booth.
- Alex feels himself growing angry with the flippant teenager there, but quickly tries to forget about it, and instead smiling at him.
- The music is piped over...Alex realizes he had forgotten how Ludovico's Technique has ruined all classical music for him.
- Crawling out of the booth sick and in pain, Alex staggers into the Korova Milkbar around the corner.
- Alex orders some laced milk, size large.
- The hallucinogens work on Alex. He starts to trip on the whole world.
- He starts to make funny noises.
- He talks about God and his Angels and Saints...and sees them standing in front of him in a sea of statues.
- He feels light, almost like he's in Heaven.
- He grows warm and cold, and collapses...
- Alex starts to cry, feeling like death may be the only answer to his sorrows.
- He doesn't know how he can kill himself without getting sick, though, as the thought of himself bloodied by his own sword makes him sick.
- Alex walks to the public library to research other methods of dying, by drifting off into a dreamless sleep.
- He flips through a medical book, but its descriptions and drawings of wounds and diseases only make him more sick.
- Then he takes down the Bible, thinking it might give him comfort like it had in the Staja days.
- But he's wrong; he starts to cry about Jews fighting with one another.
- He converses with an old man.
- A second old man recognizes Alex.
- Alex responds that he's been punished for his crime since.
- Alex is beaten up by the old men.
- Alex pleads with the attendant to protect him, and to call the police.
- The police had to beat up the old guys to disentangle Alex from them.
- OMG! Alex recognizes the older cop as old Billyboy and the younger as none other than Dim.
- Impossible, says Alex.
- Billyboy and Dim force Alex into the backseat.
- Alex can't help but wonder whether this is all a joke.
- Alex asks about Pete and says he feels sorry about Georgie.
- Alex freaks out. What's going on?
- Dim punches Alex right in the nose. Blood drips out.
- Dim and Billyboy beat Alex up. Finally, the cops drive away, leaving Alex lying there in the snow completely bloodied and disheveled.
- Alex gets up and begins walking.

- Alex stumbles upon a gate with HOME written on it. He swears he's seen this before.
- He knocks on the door; it opens.
- He tells the man he's been beaten up by the police and left to die on the road.
- Alex knows right then what was so familiar about HOME.
- Alex drinks some whiskey to warm up.
- Alex recalls the manuscript, *A Clockwork Orange*, on the table.
- Alex bathes, gets in some pajamas already laid out for him, and has supper with the writer.
- The writer speaks of repayment.
- The writer recognizes Alex from the picture in the paper.
- The man urges Alex to tell his story.
- Alex treads carefully, giving little detail about his crimes.
- The writer wants Alex to help dislodge the current overbearing Government.
- Alex agrees with the writer, but seems to be more concerned with how fervently the writer has been wiping the same dinner plate (he is washing and drying the dishes).
- Alex recalls the vivid details of that unfortunate night he raped the writer's wife and caused her death. He starts to get sick.
- Alex goes to bed.
- After a really nice night's sleep, Alex walks around in the room trying to figure out the writer's name.
- He has the fantastic idea of looking for the writer's name on a manuscript of *A Clockwork Orange*.
- He leafs through the book and wonders if F. Alexander has been made crazy by his wife's death.
- Alex wonders out loud why F. Alexander is so hot and strong against the Government.
- And what does Alex get out of this, he wonders? Can he return to his enjoyment of classical music?
- Well, F. Alexander ducks the question, and instead shows Alex an article he's written for him, soon to be published in *The Weekly Trumpet*.
- It's a long, weepy piece, but Alex is kind enough to call it "real horrorshow" to F. Alexander.
- Come again?
- Horrorshow is nadsat speak for all modern youth, Alex explains.
- Alex converses with F. Alexander's three friends who have just arrived.
- Alex starts to argue with them.
- Alex objects, crying that he doesn't want to be a plaything, an idiot that anyone could just use. After all, he's not dim.
- F. Alexander raises an eyebrow when he hears the word "dim."
- What's Dim got to do with it? Alex retorts, without thinking.
- F. Alexander goes mad.
- Alex tries to leave.
- Z. Dolin, F. Alexander's associate who is also there, grabs a hold of Alex.
- Alex is dragged into town by F. Alexander's associates.
- They arrive at an apartment, plop Alex in, and tell him that this is his new home.
- Before they leave, however, they ask Alex whether he's the person F. Alexander feared he was.
- Alex responds that he's paid for his sins.
- Alex takes a nap.

- When he wakes up, he hears Otto Skadelig's Symphony Number Three through the wall.
- Alex can enjoy it for only two seconds before the pain and sickness overcome him.
- He bangs on the wall for it to be turned off.
- He crashes against the wall until his knuckles bleed.
- He plugs his ears with his fingers – no luck!
- He bangs against the door – it is locked!
- In a frenzy, he leaps from the window stories above ground, and bids farewell to the world, "May God forgive you for a ruined life."
- He falls hard on the sidewalk.
- Before he passes out, it becomes clear to him that F. Alexander and associates were trying to force his suicide to suit their own political agenda against the Government.
- After a long time, Alex comes to, not knowing who he is or why he's been totally bandaged up. He can't feel anything.
- Alex drifts in and out of consciousness for a while.
- He comes to with Z. Dolin, Rubinstein, and D. B. da Silva there, calling him "friend" and saying how well he has served "Liberty."
- Alex protests this, but to no avail because his mouth is bandaged up.
- Alex falls into a dream, during which he's doing ultra-violent stuff like in the olden days. A little bit of smashing into a parked auto, a bit of raping young girls, and so on.
- He wakes up in a hospital with his parents by his bed.
- Alex orders them out of his room with a lot of violent profanity.
- He realizes that he can think violent thoughts and not get sick.
- He asks the nurse how long he's been there.
- Alex has her confirm that Ludovico's Technique has been reversed on him.
- More time passes and Alex gets a lot better. At 2:30pm one day, Alex receives a special visit from the Minister of the Interior, followed by a dozen of journalists and photographers.
- The two converse cryptically for a while.
- The Minister now tells Alex that he's been cured, after all, and that a high-paying job is lined up for him when he checks out. He also reminds Alex that it's the Government that ultimately put away the crazy lunatic, F. Alexander, who wants his life.
- Distracted by the thought, a photographer screams out, SMILE! and Alex complies.
- Now, the Minister brings in a present – a stereo! Alex is overjoyed.
- Beethoven's Ninth is just a signature away, they tell him.
- Alex signs, and the symphony that ensues is glorious indeed.
- Alex, and his three new friends – Len, Rick, and Bully – are drinking milk-plus at the Korova Milkbar.
- They are still dressed in the heighth of fashion.
- Randomly, but presumably feeling the drugs kick in, Alex punches some dude in the stomach and orders his friends out of the bar.
- The boys suggest grabbing a glass of hot something at the Duke of New York, not far away.
- Alex grants permission.
- Old ladies flirt with Alex for a round of freebies.
- Alex isn't feeling it, saying that his cash is hard-earned.
- Seeing how eager the old women are, he loosens up and orders them a round. He orders a small beer for himself.
- As he pulls the money out of his pockets, a newspaper clipping of a baby drops to the

floor. His entourage makes fun of him.
- Alex tears up the photo, embarrassed.
- Still not feeling it, Alex excuses himself and suggests meeting the next night.
- It is dark outside, and Alex feels just as somber. He notes that lately his down moods have been dictating what music he listens to. Instead of great, violent symphonies, he's more partial to sappy romantic songs.
- He walks into a coffeehouse for a cup of tea.
- He bumps into Pete and Georgina at the coffeehouse.
- Alex cannot believe how grown up Pete seems…and married, too!
- Alex continues to sit in the coffeehouse after the couple leaves Alex, thinking about how time has passed him by. After all, he's eighteen now, and eighteen is not such a young age anymore.
- Back out in the dark winter streets, Alex envisions his adulthood. He likes the idea of a wife, a mother to his son.
- Anyway, a wife and a son: that's something new to do, like a new chapter in a book, this book of life.
- And he resolves to do it all.

Minister of the Interior Character Analysis

The Minister of the Interior is a pragmatist, a utilitarian, or even a Machiavellian, if you will. OK, more to the point, he is an ends-justify-the-means kind of guy, or basically, Mr. Necessary Evil. Except that he doesn't see it as "evil," per se. As a high-ranking government official given the task of reforming the streets before the next election, he is interested only in results, not in people. He wants a stable society, and to achieve this, he is willing to sacrifice any principle or individual citizen for achieving that goal.

The Minister institutes the Reclamation Treatment program (which involves Ludovico's Technique) against hardened criminals. The idea is that the criminal tendencies are permanently removed forever through behavioral modifications. Against the problematic "modern youth" that plague the streets, the Minister introduces a rather creative "police program." Apparently, this program involves giving the hoodlums police badges so they can terrorize the rest of the people and turn them against individual crime. Instead, it's essentially institutionalized crime. What a guy, huh?

He readily admits to Alex that he doesn't care about individual liberties, and feels no guilt over it. After all, his only concern is the welfare of the State at large, so it would be asking too much for him to mind the details. However, he does realize that in order for the State's citizens to accept him, he has to win Alex's approval – and that, of course, is his only motivation for restoring Alex to his old self towards the end of the book.

Minister of the Interior Timeline and Summary

- Alex kills a guy in jail overnight.
- The next day, at 11am, the Governor and the Chief Warden and other important looking officials come for Alex. They chat among one another about whether the Government ought to move away from outmoded theories of dealing with criminals and embrace the new theory formed from a "curative" view.
- The Minister of the Interior, among the official-looking people, turns to the Governor and suggests that he take Alex to Dr. Brodsky, to be transformed out of recognition.
- Alex thinks those words taste like freedom.
- That evening, the guards drag Alex down to the Governor's office.
- The Governor informs him that the important man who graced his cell in the morning was the new Minister of the Interior, who apparently has odd ideas about the state reform system.
- The Governor tells Alex that he is to be "transformed" starting tomorrow by enrolling in a two-week program, overseen by the Minister, which will end in his release.
- About two weeks later, it is Alex's last day in the white building.
- The Staja Governor, the chaplain, the Minister of the Interior, the doctors, and the other white coats are present for the demonstration to come.
- The demonstration ensues.
- At the end of it, the Minister of the Interior starts to praise the system and gloats about how the Technique really works.
- Now freed, Alex sits in a coffee shop reading an article in the paper about the Institute for Reclamation of Criminal Types and Ludovico's Technique. He stumbles upon the Minister of the Interior boasting about how clever the system is.
- While Alex lies unconscious in the hospital after his jump, the Minister of the Interior apparently orders doctors to undo Ludovico's Technique on him, restoring him to his old self.
- More time passes and Alex gets a lot better. At 2:30pm one day, Alex receives a special visit from the Minister of the Interior, dressed in the height of fashion, of course, and followed by a dozen journalists and photographers.
- The Minister calls Alex a friend, but Alex calls him an enemy.
- The two converse cryptically for a while.
- The Minister now announces to Alex that he's been cured, and that a high-paying job is lined up for him when he checks out. He also reminds Alex that it was the Government that ultimately put away the crazy lunatic, F. Alexander, who wants his life.
- Distracted by the thought, a photographer screams out, SMILE! and Alex complies.
- A picture of the two looking like old friends is taken.
- Now, the Minister brings in a present for Alex – a stereo!

F. Alexander Character Analysis

Though F. Alexander is a writer-type, he can't be mistaken for an ineffective bookworm. He's a

political dissident, and one so committed to his anti-Government vision that he's willing to sacrifice any number of individuals for it, including Alex…or especially Alex. This is understandable, however, since F. Alexander did lose his wife violently earlier in the book – an incident for which he holds the Government generally responsible, and, later, Alex personally responsible. After the passing of his beloved wife, he's been devoting his entire being and purpose to…liberty? Political idealism? Or…vengeance?

F. Alexander may claim it's ideal one above the others, but one could argue a certain level of hypocrisy to this if you think about it. While he professes to want to overthrow the Government in the name of liberty, his reasons are deeply personal: his wife died at the hands of an ineffective Government. While he professes to want to help victims of the Government in the name of justice, he willingly sacrifices Alex. Where does this leave us? You be the judge.

F. Alexander Timeline and Summary

- Alex and co. barge into F. Alexander's home. At this point, F. Alexander is an anonymous writer.
- He's got the look, too, as he's wearing horn-rimmed glasses.
- The writer protests.
- Alex, picking up a pile of typewriter paper, starts to mock him. *A Clockwork Orange* is the title of the manuscript; Alex tears it up.
- At this, F. Alexander lashes out at Alex. Dim starts to beat up F. Alexander.
- Dim holds F. Alexander's wife down, while Alex begins to rip off her clothes.
- Alex rapes F. Alexander's wife. F. Alexander witnesses this, and howls the dirtiest of words at him.
- More beating by Alex and gang.
- A few years pass by…
- One night, F. Alexander opens the door to an unrecognizable Alex, who has been beaten up by the police and left to die in the countryside.
- He leads Alex in to a warm fire.
- He offers Alex some whiskey to warm up.
- He makes Alex a nice bath, and offers him a full supper.
- He recognizes Alex from his picture in the papers earlier in the morning.
- He tries to give Alex his sympathies against the government and the police.
- He urges Alex to tell his story.
- Upon hearing how Alex underwent Ludovico's Technique, F. Alexander is enraged.
- He wants Alex to join him in trying to dislodge the current overbearing Government.
- He launches into a huge speech about how ever since his wife has died, he's been having a hard time doing the chores around the house himself.
- He goes into detail about his wife's rape and murder.
- Alex starts to get sick upon hearing it, and F. Alexander orders him to bed.
- F. Alexander calls Alex to breakfast from downstairs and hands him some boiled eggs and black toast.
- He informs Alex that he's been making phone calls all morning to people who might be

interested in his case, as Alex is a "very potent weapon" against the Government in this sensitive time just before the election.
- He characterizes the Government as a brutal totalitarian regime, and says he's defending liberty, or at least the tradition of it.
- F. Alexander shows Alex an article he's written for him, soon to be published in *The Weekly Trumpet*. He wants Alex to sign his name on it.
- It's a long, weepy piece, but Alex is kind enough to call it "real horrorshow" to F. Alexander.
- Horrorshow is nadsat speak for all modern youth, Alex explains.
- F. Alexander hurries off to do the dishes.
- F. Alexander becomes suspicious because Alex's speech reminds him of someone else's speech pattern in a former life…uh oh!
- Alex says dim. Dim? F. Alexander raises an eyebrow.
- F. Alexander goes mad, shouting out loud that if this is the same coincidence that raped and killed his wife he'll tear Alex up and split him apart real good.
- D. B. da Silva tries to calm F. Alexander down.
- F. Alexander looks like a lunatic at this point, and keeps chanting Dim…dim dim dim.
- After jumping from the window of the tall building, Alex passes out on the ground, but before he does so, it becomes clear to him that F. Alexander and associates were trying to force his suicide to suit their own political agenda against the Government.
- After less than a month or so, the Minister of the Interior reveals that F. Alexander has been jailed by the Government for bordering on lunacy and for wanting to take Alex's life.

Prison Chaplain Character Analysis

The resident priest of Staja, the prison chaplain genuinely finds Alex endearing. He also likes Alex because he is a snitch, and the snitching provides fodder for the chaplain moving up in the world. A hypocrite, this religious man seems to be always drunk on Scotch and smoking cigs. What's worse, though, is that while he gets all righteous atop his sermon mount, he buries his principles and morality for his professional ambitions. He adamantly opposes the State's endorsement of Ludovico's Technique, but never speaks up against it except to Alex.

Dr. Brodsky and Dr. Branom Character Analysis

The white-coats are behavioral scientists who oversee Alex's treatment with Ludovico's Technique. Both are soulless and content with their work. They are patronizing to Alex. They are not personable. They don't understand Alex, nor do they have any interest in doing so. They see science as a form of religion. They aren't bothered one bit by Alex's inability to make moral choices. In fewer words, they may well be the soulless automatons (clockwork oranges) that Burgess opposes so vehemently.

Dim, Georgie Character Analysis

Dim and George first are members of Alex's gang. Dim is the strong and dumb one that has a problem with Alex's authority. Georgie is the smarter and ambitious one that leads the rebellion against Alex for the sake of financial gain. Both are traitors to Alex: Dim incapacitates Alex at the Manse site, leading to his arrest, and ultimately becomes a police officer, thanks to the program introduced by the Minister of the Interior. In this position, he gets even with Alex. Georgie dies in a later raid.

P.R. Deltoid Character Analysis

Post-Corrective Adviser to Alex, P. R. Deltoid is a detached State employee who nonetheless seeks to do the right thing. He takes some liking to Alex, as evidenced by his visit to Alex's home to caution Alex against trouble-making. However, Alex puzzles P. R. Deltoid because his propensity for brutality defies any logical explanation. Ultimately, though, P. R. Deltoid resents and rejects types like Alex, and spits in his face in the holding cell. His inability to understand Alex also causes P. R. Deltoid to make up lies so as to put the boy behind bars for fourteen years.

Pete Character Analysis

Pete has always been the most reasonable among Alex's entourage. Pete is significant because he represents the idea that criminals can reform on their own: the idyllic life he chooses to lead in part three is due entirely to his own efforts. Pete is also notable for being the inspiration to Alex's eventual transformation, as his happiness with his life and wife causes Alex to want the same for himself.

Character Roles

Protagonist
Alex
This is Alex's story, as told through Alex's eyes, so naturally he is the protagonist. Some say that Alex doesn't exactly encompass traditional protagonist qualities, such as being a non-evil person. We forgive him, though, as he comes to terms with actually growing up at the end. Others argue that Alex is a hero who doesn't just lie down and take it from the State – quite the opposite, he fights against what he believes is cruel and inhumane treatment. You just have to decide for yourself whether he's more evil or heroic, or whether he is in fact the ultimate anti-hero, which would be a combination of both.

Antagonist
The State / Minister of the Interior

Alex spends all of parts two and three of the book fighting against the State and its solution to eliminate violent youth. Insofar as the Minister of the Interior stands for the State or its Governmental authority, he may also be viewed as an antagonistic force.

Guide/Mentor
Prison Chaplain

The prison chaplain's whole beef with Ludovico's Technique stems from his belief that forced morality is no better than chosen evil. He is the first to caution Alex against the dangers of Ludovico's Technique, and also the first to sympathize with Alex's loss of moral choice. Although he does not guide Alex in the traditional way, his thoughts and beliefs definitely pave the way for Alex's own.

Guide/Mentor
Peter

Originally one of Alex's droogs, Peter grows up to be a responsible adult leading a "normal" and happy life. When Alex bumps into Peter and Georgina in Chapter 21, he is inspired by Pete's apparent contentment to seek out a normal life for himself. Thus, Peter can claim at least partial credit for Alex's growth and transformation.

Foil
F. Alexander

The two Alexes are completely different. Our protagonist is an anti-intellectual, believes in personal liberty, and espouses the philosophical view that man is born evil. F. Alexander, on the other hand, is a bookworm type, believes in the idea of liberty (though at the expense of individuals), and holds the noble view that people are born good only to be corrupted by the modern age.

Companions
Dim, Peter, Georgie, Len, Rick, Bully

The first three droogs make up the original gang, with Alex as leader. Dim and Georgie later defect from the gang, though, and their actions are ultimately responsible for Alex's incarceration. Dim also later becomes a total enemy of Alex's, beating him up and leaving him out to die as a way to get even. Interestingly enough, in the last chapter of the book, Alex actually looks up to Peter (see discussion "Guide/Mentor"). The last three are his new droogs, introduced in the last chapter of part three – we don't know much beyond their names.

Character Clues

Speech and Language

Contrary to what you will recall after reading the book, both nadsat and formal (or "gentlemanly") English are spoken in *A Clockwork Orange*; either can be used to characterize the speaker. For starters, nadsat is a special slang developed and used by the "modern youth," or the teens (1.3.3). The formal English, or "gentlemanly goloss," is spoken by the adults, and is particularly "formal" sounding when the authorities (Minister of the Interior, prison chaplain, and doctors) speak it. Thus, the spoken language generally divides opposing types of characters:

the young and the old, the violent and the peaceful, the helpless children and the oppressive authorities. Notably, Alex is versed in both dialects, switching between them throughout the book. This signifies that he belongs to both worlds – or, at least, that he is capable of transitioning (eventually) to the adult world.

Clothing

Although both youth and adults can dress in the "heighth of fashion" within their respective niches of society, Burgess uses clothing as a characterization tool. The nadsat teens dress in a combination of weird gaudiness, Gothicism, and gender-neutrality that makes them easily identifiable. The adults seem to dress like Communists – drab and gray, with no personality. The authority figures, on the other hand, don spiffy suits, much like modern businessmen; their clothing betrays just how important they are. Lastly, the doctors and scientists are also easily identifiable in their "white coats." In fact, in part two of the book, Alex specifically refers to the authorities exclusively as the "important suits" and the scientists as "white-coats."

Music (Knowledge v. Ignorance of)

There are those who know their stuff when it comes to music (that would be Alex, the prison chaplain, and Andy, the record store guy), and there are those who are completely ignorant of it (that would be Dim and Dr. Brodsky). Because of their expertise in and enjoyment of music, we are supposed to like and think highly of Alex, the prison chaplain, and Andy. Due to their ignorance of classical music, Dim and Dr. Brodsky are intended to be soulless and even "fatally flawed" people. For Dim, the problem is his dimness; for Dr. Brodsky, it's his lack of respect for free will and humanity.

Choice of Drink

Ayn Rand has been quoted as saying (in Atlas Shrugged), "Tell me what a man finds sexually attractive and I will tell you his entire philosophy of life." Well, for our purposes here, substitute "sexually attractive" with "choice of alcoholic beverage." Who would have known that what you choose to poison your body with is tell-tale for who or what you are? Listen up, Shmoopers. The nadsat-speaking teenagers all drink milk, a beverage for infants. Alright, so it's milk-plus hallucinogens, but nonetheless, the key substance is milk. The adults (Alex's parents, the alibi "babooschkas" at the bar, and the prison chaplain) prefer Scotch, apparently. So right off the bat we have an interesting dichotomy – a fine alcoholic line.

Literary Devices

Symbols, Imagery, Allegory

Cigarettes

Known as "cancers" in nadsat, cigarettes are what the characters puff on when they need to appear cool or nonchalant (in the case of the "modern youth"), when they are being philosophical or anxious (in the case of the prison chaplain and Rex, the cop driving Dim and Billyboy's getaway squad car), or just delinquent (the ten-year-old girls Alex rapes, all the kids at the bars, as well as Alex's entourage). What is interesting is how Burgess calls them

"cancers," obviously to incite the negative connotation.

"HOME"
The sign hanging on the gate of the country cottage where F. Alexander and wife reside also has real significance. In part one, Alex and co. stumble upon the cottage seeking a violent, fun time. Their actions directly threaten all positive connections of a "home." In part three, as Alex stumbles upon the same country cottage after he being left out to die by Dim and Billyboy, "home" comes to symbolize a place of refuge, solace, and a meeting of minds (between Alex and F. Alexander) against the Government.

Breasts or "Groodies"
In nadsat, breasts are called "groodies." All the girls and women (other than the ten-year-olds) have them. They seem to make the boys wild with desire. Well, at least this is true for Alex, since he's the only source we have, and he does talk incessantly about them hanging out of every woman's shirt, and their pink nipples waving hello at him, he is thereby caused to have the urge to do the old in-out-in-out. So, they very obviously symbolize femininity and sexuality; and, in Alex's case, a rape-to-come.

Milk
Everyone at the Korova Milkbar drinks milk. Alex drinks milk with almost every meal. Yet, none of the adults seem to be drinking it. Hmm… Could this mean that the milk-drinking teenagers are bunch of babies? You bet. Here associated with the naïve and immature, milk is the substance for infants – unsophisticated and helpless. For the "modern youth" that nurse on the stuff laced with hallucinogens, the explanation is that they are young people who have chosen to add poison to their otherwise innocent slates, making them the evil youth that they are.

Vellocet, Synthemesc, Drencrom
From the text, we infer that these are hallucinogens added to the milk – a popular drink for the modern youth. Symbolizing evil, these are the poisons the kids choose to be exposed to. While under the influence of these poisons, the youth act out violently and brutally as urchins.

Blood
Alex revels in his descriptions of the red, hot blood that oozes or gushes or pours out from his victims. To him, blood is beauty; he experiences aesthetic joy from the blood he sheds. Considering Alex's violent tendencies, and insofar as Alex delights in destruction, blood also comes to symbolize vitality and energy.

Night and Darkness
Alex identifies with the night and all things associated with it. According to him, so do the other "modern youth," since they rule the streets at night. Night and darkness represent a sort of security and privacy that Alex and other modern youth crave. Perhaps because they can't be seen or found as easily; perhaps because it heightens the feeling of anonymity. Either way, as a setting, it certainly enables crime.

Day and Lightness
Alex contrasts night and darkness with day and lightness. Day and lightness are for the "starry folks." Patrol cars are more abundant on the streets and security is ensured. There is nowhere

to hide where sun and light are present, as in the case of the holding cell and interrogation room. Alex feels extremely exposed and vulnerable in the day and in lightness. These are not his elements.

Ludvig van Beethoven, Wolfgang Amadeus Mozart, Handel

The Classical composers represent all that is ideal to and sacred for Alex, as these composers have created the highest and purest form of art, and therefore joy, for Alex. The fact that one or more of their compositions almost always accompanies Alex's perpetrating a certain crime – which he often commits for sheer aesthetics or sensory bliss – also bodes well for our interpretation.

Broken Elevator

The broken elevator in Alex's parents' Flatblock represents societal and moral demise. Indeed, it symbolizes everything that is wrong with the society that Alex lives in. The predictability of its lack of functionality suggests that the societal decay is nothing new and that it's here to stay for a long while.

Setting

A not-so-distant future city or town in England.

Considering that the novel was written in the 1960s, we're probably well past the dystopian futuristic setting Burgess envisioned for this work. Come to think of it, though, what constitutes the "heighth of fashion" in this work is still a bit more futuristic (read: bizarre) than what we've seen in our time, so maybe give another tack on another twenty years to imagine when that "future" ought to occur. It is worth noting how the macabre and filthy streets add to the "sensation" of this being a gross, dystopian city in the future, though.

Narrator Point of View

First Person (Alex)

We only get what Alex hands us, so be mindful of both the perspective and biases inherent to a first-person narrative. The advantage to this is that we get extremely intimate with and engaged in Alex's life. After all, it's an "insider's view" we're seeing, albeit from only one lens. Despite all of the senseless brutality he inflicts upon others, for example, we come to like and forgive Alex, because we see how immature and naïve he is. The disadvantage is that we aren't privy to how others view our protagonist-narrator (except when it's obvious – like when P. R. Deltoid spits on Alex's face), and so we can't be exactly fair or just in our assessment of each situation.

Genre

Dystopian Literature; Coming-Of-Age; Horror; Satire

The beauty of *A Clockwork Orange* is that it has its feet on four boats: dystopian novel, coming-of-age story, horror flick, and political satire. Arguably, there's a fifth philosophical commentary boat that could also claim admission. From the top: it is a dystopian novel because it takes place in the future, and everything is dark, eerie, violent, and headed down a sad and non-utopian path. It is a coming-of-age story because of the trials and transformation Alex endures. The horror aspect of the work cannot be clearer amidst all the beating, teeth-plucking, eye-gouging, mugging, and raping that occurs. The satiric aspect comes through in the novel's political commentary. Finally, amidst all that debate about moral choice, free will, personal freedom, and behavioral modification, Burgess conveys a real anti-totalitarian message in this novel.

Tone

Angst-ridden, irreverent, but detached and matter-of-fact

A Clockwork Orange is almost a foreign-language work because it is not written in British, American, or standard English; it features nadsat, a made up language incorporating elements of Cockney and Russian spoken by the "modern youth" in the book. Figuring out what Alex means with each term is a feat in itself, and it takes a few chapters for even the most astute reader to get a firm grip on the language. Now, once you think you've crossed the language barrier, the tone will be easy to gauge. Alex is a matter-of-fact kind of narrator, although he does embellish some of the goings-on for dramatic effect (this shouldn't be surprising because nadsat employs a decent amount of onomatopoeia, or the use of words that *sound* like what they mean). Much of the tone is irreverent and immature-sounding. We also detect considerable angst, not surprising given the subject matters being described. Interestingly enough, however, the tone Alex uses when describing violence might be described as almost detached. He very matter-of-factly recounts exactly what punches he throws and just how much blood oozes out from his victims' orifices.

Writing Style

Clever, playful

As we discussed under "Tone," Burgess' clever and unique style owes much to his use of nadsat, which has its fair share of onomatopoeia to clue us in on what is being said (those of us who aren't experts in Russian or the Cockney accent, at least). For instance, the very second sentence of chapter one shows just how clever the text as a whole can be: "There was me, that is Alex, and my three droogs, that is Pete, Georgie, and Dim, Dim being really dim, and we sat in the Korova Milkbar making up our rassoodocks what to do with the evening, a flip dark chill winter bastard though dry" (1.1.2). From the context, we may reliably infer that "droog" must

mean "friend" or "companion;" Dim "being really dim" is suitably cute; and "flip dark chill winter bastard though dry" sounds like some free-association wordplay on what a "winter evening" ought to feel like. Burgess doesn't explicate, but we know exactly what he means. Simply clever.

What's Up With the Title?

Superficially, "a clockwork orange" was just some lingo that author Anthony Burgess overheard among old Londoners. In Anthony Burgess's own words in the introduction entitled "A Clockwork Orange Resucked," the title refers to a person who "has the appearance of an organism lovely with colour and juice but is in fact only a clockwork toy to be wound up by God or the Devil or (since this is increasingly replacing both) the Almighty State." In other words, and again Burgess's own, it stands for the "application of a mechanistic morality to a living organism oozing with juice and sweetness." So, basically, it refers to a person who is robotic behaviorally but one that is, in all other respects, human. The title is significant not only because Burgess references it about, say, 1,000 times throughout the book, but also because it sums up what threatened our protagonist-narrator so much. Oops. Did that get your attention?

What's Up With the Ending?

The ending, or the 21st chapter of the book, provides closure to the book for some readers. In fact, this is the only chapter where our protagonist-narrator experiences growth, or more profoundly, personal transformation. In fact, we dare say that given his newfound discontent with violence and violent music, and interest in forging a family, Alex is all grown up. Structurally, it balances out the other two parts of the book, each with seven chapters. Thematically, it comes full-circle, starting off with the same question and description combination as chapter one in part one of the book, but closing the loop with Alex rejecting the person he was at the commencement of his journey and looking forward to a new kind of life.

That would be the easy interpretation. In the United States, and for 24 years, this 21st chapter was left out of all published versions of *A Clockwork Orange*. In fact, Americans were so content with the extremely open-ended ending provided by the 20th chapter that no one bothered to look on eBay for a British edition of the work. (OK, so eBay wasn't around in the 80s, but hey, same idea.) What's even more interesting is that Stanley Kubrick's famous (and forever memorialized) film adaptation of the book was modeled after the twenty-chapter version, so why is the 21st chapter even necessary?

Burgess hints at the answer to this, suggesting that politics or different regional aesthetics had something to do with leaving out the 21st chapter. Perhaps it's because the 20th chapter, with evil prancing all over the page, is sexier. Perhaps optimism as embodied by the 21st chapter is at odds with the rest of the work. We have millions of theories, as do Burgess and the publisher responsible for nixing the 21st chapter in the American edition, but at the end of the day, you'll have to decide for yourself whether you prefer it one way or the other. Just be ready to justify your opinion.

Did You Know?

Trivia

- *A Clockwork Orange* was initially published in 1962. In the United States, the book was published with only twenty chapters. Elsewhere in the world, the book had twenty chapters. Apparently, this was the doing of Anthony Burgess's American editor, and Burgess has yet to get over his bad judgment. He chews out his publisher in an introduction he writes for the book's second release in 1986. The publisher could do nothing but retreat and apologize.
- *A Clockwork Orange* is Anthony Burgess' least favorite of the many books he has penned. In fact, he would disown it if he could, much like Beethoven is rumored to have wished to disown Minuet in G, if he could.
- The term "hypnopaedia" was also used in another dystopian novel, *Brave New World*, published by Aldous Huxley thirty years prior to Burgess's publication of *A Clockwork Orange*.
- The clothes at the "heighth of fashion" for some of the modern youth are still considered to be at the height of fashion today.

Steaminess Rating

R

To justify the R rating, let us quickly reference the following: "… real good horrorshow groodies they were that then exhibited their pink glazzies, O my brothers, while I untrussed and got ready for the plunge" (1.2.23). Alex is getting ready to rape the woman who has that pair of lovely breasts with their pink nipples. This narrative occurs just before Alex takes the "plunge" while Dim holds the woman down. And while the woman's husband watches. What? Horrible, did you say? You ain't seen nothin' yet. Does it get more sexual and violent than this, you ask? Read your book and find out.

Allusions and Cultural References

Literature, Philosophy, and Mythology
Aristotle (1.1.8)
P. B. Shelley (1.1.26)

Historical References
Henry VIII (1.1.26)

Pop Culture
Berti Laski (1.1.10)
Elvis Presley (1.1.26)
Jonny Zhivago (1.3.3)
Friedrich Gitterfenster (1.3.3)
Geoffrey Plautus (1.3.26)
Mozart (1.3.28, 3.2.2, 3.2.6, 3.6.74, 3.7.52)
J. S. Bach (1.3.28, 2.1.9, 2.1.23)
Claudius Birdman (1.4.24)
Ludwig van Beethoven (1.4.24. 1.4.26, 1.4.34, 1.5.30, 1.6.14, 1.6.15, 1.7.15, 2.2.11, 2.6.3,
2.6.5, 2.6.19, 3.2.6, 3.5.13, 3.6.74, 3.6.76)
G. F. Handel (2.1.9, 2.2.11, 2.6.19)
Adrian Schweigselber (2.1.12)
Otto Skadelig (3.5.41)
Arthur Schoenberg (3.6.74)
Carl Orff (3.6.74)
Felix Mendelsohhn (3.7.52)

Best of the Web

Movie or TV Productions
A Clockwork Orange, Stanley Kubrick, 1971
http://www.imdb.com/title/tt0066921/
A screenplay adapted from the book by Stanley Kubrick

Bananes Mecaniques, Jean-Francois Davey, 1973
http://www.imdb.com/title/tt0167020/
A copycat version including sex with goats and soundtrack by death metal

An Examination of Stanley Kubrick's A Clockwork Orange, John Musilli, 1972
http://www.imdb.com/title/tt1055280/
Talk-show with Anthony Burgess himself

Great Bolshy Yarblockos! Making A Clockwork Orange, Gary Leva, 2007
http://www.imdb.com/title/tt1147556/
Documentary of the making of A Clockwork Orange

WarnerBros Site
http://kubrickfilms.warnerbros.com/
WB Site devoted to Stanley Kubrick's films

Audios
Audio Interview with Anthony Burgess
http://wiredforbooks.org/anthonyburgess/
Don Swaim interviews Burgess

Images
Movie poster
http://www.impawards.com/1971/posters/clockwork_orange.jpg
This is supposed to be Alex Burgess

Movie still
http://www-tc.pbs.org/wgbh/cultureshock/flashpoints/theater/images/clockwork_big.jpg?mii=1
Here is Alex being strapped into the dentist's chair looking frightened of the films he's supposed to watch

Collage of movie stills
http://img5.allocine.fr/acmedia/rsz/434/x/x/x/medias/nmedia/18/36/25/34/18754532.jpg
This basically summarizes it

Doll
http://www.toytokyo.com/productImages/5374_1.jpg
Collectible 12" figure doll of Alex Burgess!

Film Review Poster
http://www.megacalendars.com/images/big/A%20Clockwork%20Orange%20AC094.jpg
Poster of a film review of the Kubrick movie

Clockwork Orange Beetle!
http://vwkombi.com/photos/beetle-bash-bug-jam-etc/Images/11.jpg
The Clockwork Orange mobile

Art Poster
http://www.modern-canvas-art.com/ekmps/shops/robboweb1/images/clockwork_orange_canvas_art.jpg
Modern ink and canvas art

Documents
The International Anthony Burgess Foundation
http://www.anthonyburgess.org/
All you ever wanted to know about Anthony Burgess

Anthony Burgess Newsletter / Zine
http://bu.univ-angers.fr/EXTRANET/AnthonyBURGESS/ABNews.html
Annually from 1999 - 2004

A Prophetic and Violent Masterpiece

http://www.city-journal.org/html/16_1_oh_to_be.html
Theodore Dalrymple on *A Clockwork Orange*

Interview
http://www.theparisreview.com/viewinterview.php/prmMID/3994
Interview of Anthony Burgess by John Cullinan at *The Paris Review*

New York Times on Anthony Burgess
http://www.nytimes.com/books/97/11/30/home/burgess.html
From the archives

Websites
Clockwork Orange: Clothing Retailers in Northern Ireland
http://www.clockwork-orange.net/
Alternative clothing being sold by the same name!

Printed in Great Britain
by Amazon